A Primer on Corporate Governance

A Primer on Corporate Governance

Spain

Félix J. López-Iturriaga
Fernando A. Tejerina-Gaite

BEP BUSINESS EXPERT PRESS

A Primer on Corporate Governance: Spain

First published in 2014 by
Business Expert Press, LLC
222 East 46th Street, New York, NY 10017
www.businessexpertpress.com

ISBN-13: 978-1-60649-760-9 (paperback)
ISBN-13: 978-1-60649-761-6 (e-book)

Business Expert Press Corporate Governance Collection

Collection ISSN: 1948-0407 (print)
Collection ISSN: 1948-0415 (electronic)

Cover and interior design by Exeter Premedia Services Private Ltd., Chennai, India

First edition: 2014

10 9 8 7 6 5 4 3 2 1

Printed in the United States of America.

Abstract

Spain has a civil law-based legal system in which court decisions are not a source of law but are of interpretative value. Also, it is a member of the European Union (EU) and as such follows the standards set out by EU directives and regulations. The privatization of large state-owned firms, liberalization, integration with EU, and the launch of the euro have all contributed to the transformation of Spain's financial system into a modern market.

Spain is considered a bank-oriented financial system in which banks play an active role relative to markets. The close link between banks and the governance of nonfinancial firms dates back to the first stages in the process of industrialization in Spain. Thereinafter banks have had close relationships with nonfinancial companies, both through lending and through stock. Currently, the Spanish financial system is going through a process of deep restructuring and consolidation. This process has not affected the outstanding role played by banks and their close ties with the governance of nonfinancial firms. Banks in Spain are not only creditors, but also reference shareholders or sit on the board of directors of nonfinancial firms.

The Spanish securities market has undergone a deep process of change and growth over the last two decades too. Technical, operating, and organization systems that support the market today have allowed important investment flows and provided the markets with greater transparency, liquidity, and efficiency. Nowadays, Spanish stock market is highly concentrated with a relatively small number of players in the utility, telecommunications, banking, construction, and energy industries.

Because of the bank orientation, the corporate governance system relies heavily on the so-called internal mechanisms of governance: the ownership structure and the board of directors. The external mechanisms of control, basically the market for corporate control, are less important than in the Anglo-Saxon environment. The low number of listed companies, the usually concentrated ownership structure, and the implementation of some control-enhancing mechanism as means to increase the control power of the main shareholder along with the relatively illiquidity of the market reduce the functioning of the market for corporate control.

In any case, the landscape of corporate governance in Spain is changing since the Spanish government has recently appointed a special committee for the reform of the corporate governance in the country. The conclusions and suggestions of this committee are likely to translate into forthcoming laws or even a new Code of Good Governance.

Keywords

board of directors, corporate finance, corporate governance, Europe, market for corporate control, ownership structure, Spain

Contents

List of Figures

List of Tables

Preface

Corporate governance has become a worldwide phenomenon, particularly after the recent economic and financial crisis. Currently, almost all countries are revising their corporate governance practices with a growing interest in the analysis of adequate directions for worldwide corporate governance reform.

This book provides a complete overview of corporate governance elements in Spain. Our survey reviews the recent evolution of the Spanish corporate governance system and highlights the main guidelines for its restructuring process. Thus, we target a broad audience of academia—practitioners and policy makers.

After our introduction, Chapter 2 presents two of the main features of the Spanish institutional context: its legal background and its orientation. Concerning the legal framework, Spain has a civil law system in which court decisions are not a source of law but are of interpretative value. In addition, Spain is a member of the European Union (EU) and, as such, follows the standards set out by EU directives and regulations. The privatization of large state-owned firms, economic and financial liberalization, the integration in the EU, and launch of the euro currency have all contributed to the modernization of Spain's financial system.

Spain is considered a bank-oriented financial system in which banks play an active role relative to markets. The close link between banks and the governance of nonfinancial firms dates back to the early stages of Spanish industrialization. Banks have maintained close relations with nonfinancial companies and are not only creditors, but also reference shareholders or seated at the board of directors of these firms. Currently the Spanish banking system is going through a process of deep restructuring and consolidation that has not affected the outstanding role played by banks and their close ties with the governance of nonfinancial firms.

In addition, the Spanish capital markets have undergone a deep process of change and growth over the last two decades. Technical, operating, and organizational systems that support the market today have allowed important investment flows and provided the markets with greater transparency, liquidity, and efficiency.

Due to the bank orientation, the corporate governance system relies heavily on the so-called internal mechanisms of governance (Chapter 3). Unlike market-oriented economies, the corporate ownership structure in Spain tends to be concentrated so the main governance problem is likely to arise between major and minor shareholders. This leads to the prevalence of one-tier boards with a high presence of owner directors.

As far as stock markets are concerned, there is concentration on a relatively small number of players in the utility, telecommunications, banking, construction, and energy industries. Thus, the external mechanisms of control (Chapter 4)—primarily the market for corporate control—are less important than in the Anglo-Saxon environment. The low number of listed companies, the usually concentrated ownership structure, and the implementation of some control-enhancing mechanism as means to increase the control power of the main shareholder (along with the relatively illiquidity of the market) reduce the functioning of the market for corporate control.

The landscape of corporate governance in Spain is shifting since the Spanish government recently appointed a special committee for the reform of the corporate governance in the country. We expect that the conclusions and suggestions of this committee will translate into forthcoming laws or even a new Code of Good Governance coherently with the international renewal of corporate governance.

CHAPTER 1

Introduction

1.1 Foundations of Corporate Governance

As Bloomfield (2013) states, corporate governance has been the single most significant issue on the business agenda internationally and globally for the past 30 or more years. Both in the academia, the politics and the practitioner's arena, new initiatives constantly arise in order to improve and strengthen how corporations are governed. One could invoke two types of reasons to explain the worldwide diffusion of this concern: The increasing importance of capital markets and the growing concern of political authorities, partially as a response to managerial excesses that led to the financial crisis.

According to the World Federation of Exchanges, in 1990 there were 21,033 quoted companies in capital markets all over the world, and 46,674 companies in 2012. The same source shows that the world market capitalization increased from US$11.8 billion in 1990 to US$58 billion in 2012. This evolution can be seen in Figure 1.1.

Given the widespread flourishing of corporate governance, there are a number of definitions. One of the most cited is the one contained in the Cadbury Report (1992), according to which corporate governance is the system by which companies are directed and controlled. It is a pioneering and very general definition, so that different regulatory bodies and authors have provided complementary definitions. In this vein, the Organization for the Economic Cooperation and Development released, in 2004, the Principles of Corporate Governance, which conceives the corporate governance as a set of relationships between a company's management, its board, its shareholders, and other stakeholders that also provides the structure through which the objectives of the company are set, and the means of attaining those objectives and monitoring performance are determined.

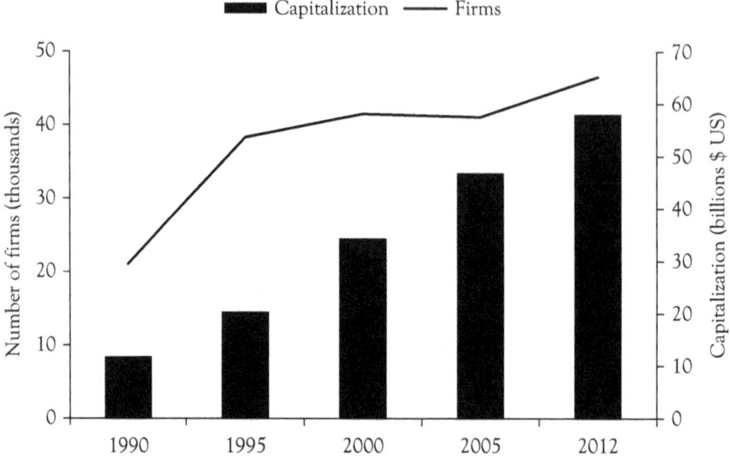

Figure 1.1 Number of quoted firms and market capitalization worldwide

Source: World Federation of Exchanges (n.d.).
Note: Annual statistics.

From an academic point of view, Shleifer and Vishny (1997) understand corporate governance as the ways in which suppliers of finance to corporations assure themselves of getting a return on their investment. It implies a clear financial approach to the topic and allows dividing the mechanisms of corporate governance into two broad groups: the internal mechanisms and the external ones. The internal mechanisms have to do with the relationships and incentives within the company (primarily the board of directors and the equity ownership of the firm), whereas the external mechanisms are related to the means that outside parties have to influence the control of the firm (namely, the market for corporate control and the legal and regulatory system).

This way of understanding the corporate governance concerns a number of constituencies such as the managers, the directors, the shareholders, and other stakeholders. Nevertheless, to effectively understand this set of relationships it cannot be removed from the contextual issues that shape the corporate governance. Research has suggested some of these underlying factors which explain how corporate governance regimes vary across countries. Among these factors, the institutional issues such as the legal tradition, the capital markets, and the accounting rules play an outstanding role. Some of these factors are reviewed in the next section.

1.2 Institutional Elements of Corporate Governance

Obviously, the optimal combination of external and internal mechanisms of corporate governance is deeply affected by the institutional architecture of each country. Financial systems have been traditionally divided into two main groups on the basis of their orientation or the weight of financial intermediation (Allen and Gale 2001). There is a continental or bank-oriented system in which money flows from ultimate creditors to ultimate debtors through financial institutions. In this system, financial intermediaries play a critical role; it is the system predominant in Japan and a number of continental European countries, such as Germany, France, Italy, or Spain. On the contrary, there is also an Anglo-Saxon or market-oriented system in which money is directly channeled by capital markets instead of financial intermediaries (the United Kingdom, the United States, and others).

Levine (2002) remarks the positive role of banks in acquiring information about firms and managers and thereby improving corporate governance. The bank-based view also stresses the shortcomings of markets because they create a myopic investor climate that reduces the incentives for long-run relationships between firms and financial intermediaries. In contrast, the market-based view highlights the role of markets in enhancing corporate governance by easing takeovers and making it easier to tie managerial compensation to firm performance. This view also underlines how financial markets can facilitate risk management.

A special case of the financial services view is the so-called Law and Finance approach (La Porta et al. 1998). According to these authors, bank versus market centeredness is not an especially useful way to distinguish financial systems. Furthermore, a well-functioning legal system facilitates the operation of both markets and intermediaries. It is the legal system that determines the overall level and quality of financial services. This approach inaugurates what Denis and McConnell (2003) call the second generation of research on corporate governance.

This second generation differs from the first one because of its international approach. The first generation of corporate governance research examines individual governance mechanisms—particularly board composition and equity ownership—in individual countries. On the contrary, the second generation of international corporate governance research recognizes the fundamental impact of differing legal systems on the structure and effectiveness of corporate governance and compares systems across countries. According to this view, the ways in which corporate finance and corporate governance evolve in a country are closely related to how this country's laws protect investor rights and how the laws are enforced in the country.

The starting point of the Law and Finance approach is the recognition that laws in different countries are typically transplanted from a few legal families or traditions. Broadly speaking, the laws come from two traditions: common law, which is English in origin; and civil law, which derives from Roman law. Within the civil tradition, there are even three major families: French, German, and Scandinavian. Civil-law countries use statutes and comprehensive codes as primary means of ordering legal material, and rely heavily on legal scholars. On the contrary, the common law is formed by judges, and precedents from judicial decisions—as opposed to contributions by scholars—shape common law. The French and the German civil traditions, as well as the common-law tradition, have spread around the world through a combination of conquest, imperialism, and imitation.

Creditor and shareholder rights, the enforcement of the law, the quality of the accountancy, the ownership concentration and per capita income show remarkable differences among groups of countries. For instance, the best protection of investors can be found in the common-law system, whereas the worst protection comes from the French system. The Scandinavian system and common-law system are also the most effective ones regarding the enforcement of the law and the quality of the accountancy.

The different legal origin leads to different corporate governance problems in each system (Azofra 2004). La Porta et al. (1998) show that the high ownership concentration is a response to the lack of legal protection. Although some ownership concentration can act as an incentive mechanism, some dispersion of ownership is also desirable to diversify risk. Poor investor protection in French civil law countries is associated with extremely concentrated ownership.

Enriques and Volpin (2007) provide some descriptive statistics about the ownership structure of quoted companies in five countries (Table 1.1).

Table 1.1 Corporate ownership concentration

	Dispersed ownership	**Pyramidal control**	**Mean largest blockholder**
France	60	15	20
Germany	50	20	57
Italy	20	20	55
United Kingdom	100	0	10
United States	80	0	5

Source: Enriques and Volpin (2007).
Note: Data in percentage.

Coherently, with the different ownership concentration, firms in common law countries (i.e., the United Kingdom and the United States) show more dispersed ownership than their civil-law counterparts. This more concentrated ownership along with the use of some control-enhancing mechanisms such as pyramidal control allow the large shareholders to make up for the poorer legal protection in civil-law countries.

CHAPTER 2

The Spanish Institutional Context

2.1 Background: The Inherited System

The recent literature on financial economics emphasizes how the financial system interacts with the mechanisms of corporate governance and with the performance of the firms. In this framework, the size of the banking sector and the size and liquidity of the stock market are related to the ownership structure of the firms and thus, to the way in which the control of the firms is exerted.

As stated in Chapter 1, countries have been traditionally classified into two groups on the basis of the orientation of the financial system: Bank-oriented versus market-oriented system. But what explains the differences in the financial systems of the countries? The most widely accepted theory is the timing of industrialization. In the countries where this process started earlier (e.g., the United Kingdom), firms were able to finance new investment gradually with internally generated funds or with securities issued in relatively developed financial markets. However, firms in countries whose industrialization started later (e.g., Spain) faced a double disadvantage relative to their advanced competitors in early industrializing ones. First, internally generated funds were not large enough relative to the important amount needed for investments in new technologies and infrastructures. Second, it was difficult to raise market funds because securities markets were underdeveloped. In this case, only banks could gather the large sums of capital required, take the risks involved in such process, and monitor their investments. Once established, bank-based systems have a strong survival capacity.

2.2 The Spanish Financial System

Spain has been traditionally seen as a country with a bank-oriented financial system (Gonzalo Angulo 2004). In spite of the general trend among developed countries toward a more market-oriented system, banks and other financial intermediaries are yet the core of the Spanish financial system. To provide a broad idea of the Spanish system, we report some descriptive data. Most of the information comes from the comprehensive survey gathered by Beck et al. (2001).

The first set of data on which we base our comparison concerns the orientation of the financial system, that is, the banks versus markets dichotomy. Consistent with Beck et al. (2001), we first calculate the overall size of the Spanish financial system, both in terms of banks and markets. Our definition of *overall size* is the result of scaling by Gross Domestic Product (GDP) the sum of bank assets and stock market capitalization. To measure the size of the banking sector we have defined *Bank assets/GDP* as the ratio of the total domestic assets of deposit money banks scaled by GDP. The size of markets is measured by the stock market capitalization as a share of GDP.[1] Based on these measures, we compute the mean value for different groups of countries: The G7, the European countries, the former 15 members of the European Union, and the group of upper middle income countries to which Spain is supposed to belong.

As shown in Figure 2.1, Spain can be considered similar to most of the other European countries in terms of the size of the financial system. Although a bit smaller than the most developed G7 countries (1.27 against 1.55), it is larger than the other upper middle income nations. The right hand columns in Figure 2.1 give some clues about the orientation of the financial system, showing a more active role of banks relative to markets. This is consistent with the traditional wisdom of Spain as a bank-oriented economy. Nevertheless, the evolution in latest years reported in Figure 2.2 shows that markets are more and more important relative to banks. With the exception of the 2001–2002 breakdown of capital markets (due to the crash of the dot-com and technological firms), the ratio of bank assets-to-market capitalization has fallen from

[1] We have also calculated the ratio of bank assets to stock market capitalization as an indicator of bank vs. markets orientation.

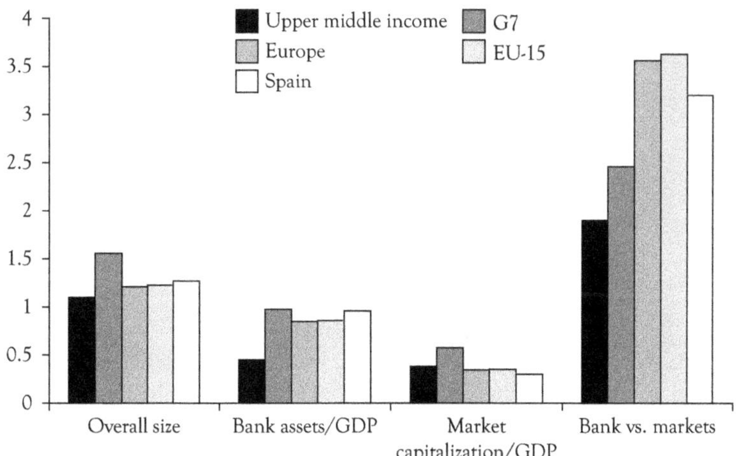

Figure 2.1 Size and orientation of the Spanish financial system

Source: Beck et al. (2001).
Notes: Overall size is the ratio of bank assets plus market capitalization to GDP. Bank versus market is the ratio of bank assets-to-market capitalization.

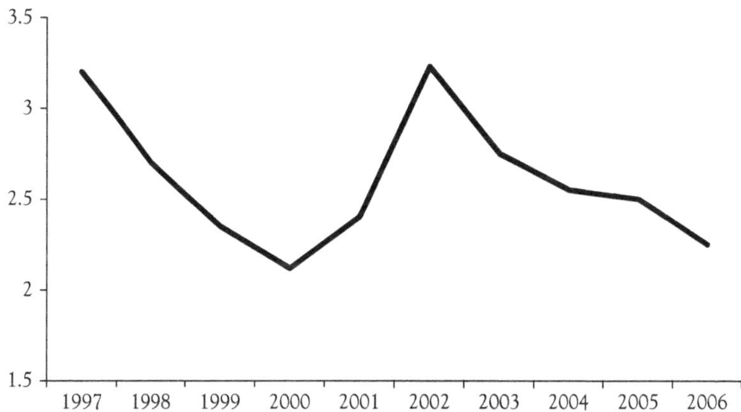

Figure 2.2 Bank assets-to-market capitalization ratio

Sources: Bank of Spain (http://www.bde.es/bde/en/) and Madrid Stock Exchange (http://www.bolsamadrid.es/ing/aspx/Portada/Portada.aspx).

3.2 to 2.2. This corroborates for Spain (as for other developed countries) the financial disintermediation or the trend to enhance capital markets relative to financial intermediaries.

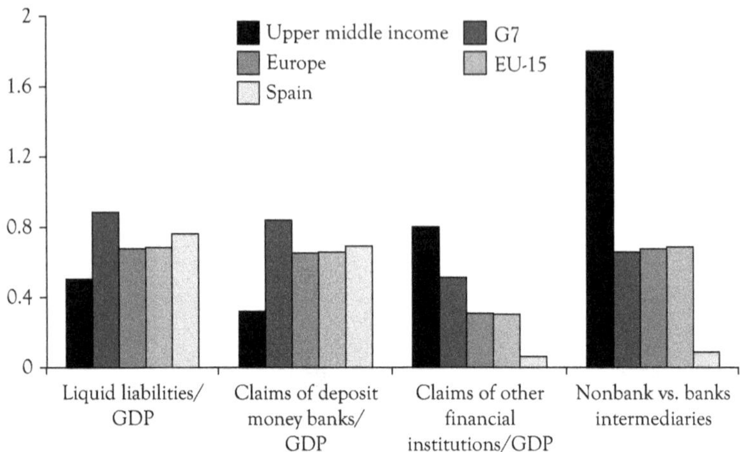

Figure 2.3 Financial intermediaries in Spain and international comparison (I)

Source: Demirgüc-Kunt and Levine (2001).
Notes: Overall size is the ratio of bank assets plus market capitalization to GDP. Bank versus market is the ratio of bank assets-to-market capitalization.

Focusing on the outstanding role of banks, we define three measures of financial intermediaries. First, *Liquid liabilities/GDP* is defined as the ratio of liquid liabilities of bank and nonbank intermediaries to GDP. It is supposed to be informative about the overall size of financial intermediaries relative to the size of the economy. Second, *Claims of deposit money banks/GDP* equals deposit money bank credits to the private sector as a share of GDP. This variable is a general indicator of bank activity in the private sector. Finally, *Claims of other financial institutions/GDP* is the ratio of nonbank credits to GDP and provides a broad measure of nonbank activity in the private sector.

Figure 2.3 is quite informative about how financial intermediation is performed by banks and other financial institutions. One can see that the size of financial intermediaries in Spain (measured through liquid liabilities) is near the international mean value (0.76 in Spain against 0.88 in the G7 countries and 0.67 in European countries). On the contrary, nonbank intermediaries are much less important in Spain than in the other countries (0.06 against 0.51 and 0.30, respectively). More

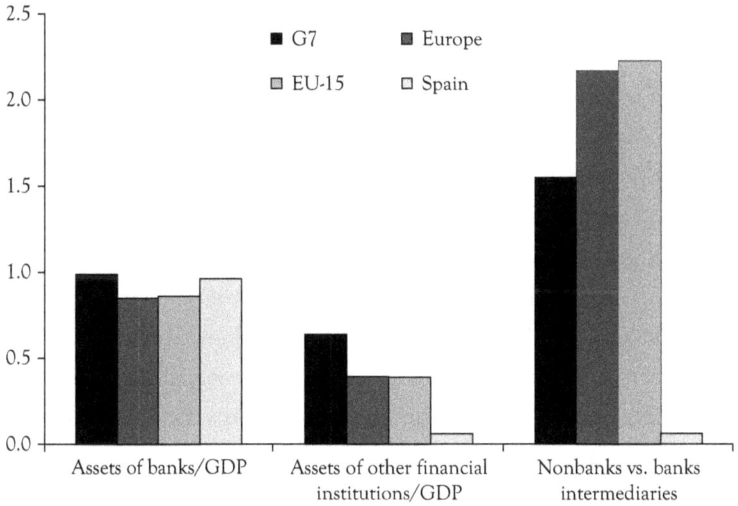

Figure 2.4 Financial intermediaries in Spain and international comparison (II)

Source: Demirgüc-Kunt and Levine (2001).

interestingly, when we compare the size of deposit money banks with the size of other financial intermediaries (right hand columns in Figure 2.3), we see that the large size of intermediaries in Spain is due basically to the bank sector rather than to other financial institutions.

If we compare banks and nonbank intermediaries in terms of assets instead of claims (Figure 2.4), the results confirm previous ideas: The assets of the Spanish banks are close to other countries but the assets owned by other financial institutions are anomalously low, so that there is an unambiguous leading role of banks as the most important type of financial intermediary in Spain. This is the main reason to provide a more indepth explanation of the Spanish banking system and the net of relationships between nonfinancial firms and banks in Spain.

2.2.1 The Spanish Banking System

Privatization of large State-owned firms, liberalization, integration with European Union, and the launch of the euro have all contributed to the transformation of Spain's financial system into a modern market. However, after a decade of rapid growth, Spain entered a severe recession in 2007, which was triggered by the global crisis but has been reinforced by sharp domestic adjustment already underway, caused mainly by the oversized residential construction industry. The crisis has accelerated reforms in the financial systems, with significant changes in the banking system.

Two of the most meaningful features of the Spanish banking system are the heterogeneous kind of legal status of banks, and the close link between banks and the governance of nonfinancial firms. Regarding the legal status, in Spain there are three main banking institutions: commercial banks, savings banks, and credit cooperatives. The commercial banks are clearly stockholder oriented, whereas savings banks are private foundations, with a board of trustees with representatives from regional authorities, city halls, workers, depositors, and the founding entity. Savings banks are a quite specific institution in the Spanish financial system with no formal owners and no market for corporate control of them. Credit cooperatives are mainly located in rural areas and have a secondary role.

In spite of the differences in the legal status among them, they compete under equal conditions in the loan, deposit, and financial service markets. There are no operational differences, and regulations are the same for the three types, as well as their accounting practices, external reporting, and credit-risk management standards.

Spanish commercial banks are privately owned and publicly traded on the stock exchange. After the intense process of mergers and acquisitions during the 1990s, Banco Bilbao Vizcaya Argentaria (BBVA) and Banco Santander (BS) emerged as the two key players. In 2010, they were among the world's top 15 banks (Dalton and Daily 2001). As a result, there is a high concentration in the industry, with BBVA and Santander accounting for around 80 percent of the country's commercial banking assets.

As far as savings banks are concerned, not long ago they seemed to be very successful. They had an impressive and growing market share of approximately 50 percent and by and large were so profitable and efficient that one would not be able to see any difference in their performance compared with the private banks, including the Spanish giants Santander and BBVA. In a publication by the European Savings Banks Institute, Manghetti (2011) even called them a model of successful savings banks. However, this has drastically changed in recent years. The ups and downs of the Spanish savings banks in the past two decades can be traced back to the reform that started after Spain's integration to European Union in 1986 and occurred under the pressure of the European Union, which was strongly opposed to publicly owned banks.

Until the 1970s, the Spanish savings banks had been public institutions. As such they had always been exposed to political interventions, and their activities were restricted to narrowly defined areas and in terms of which operations they could undertake. There were many local savings banks, and they were small and not particularly efficient institutions. With the reforms and the economic liberalization that began in the seventies, they were reshaped to become modern financial institutions. They were privatized, the regional principle was abolished and they were granted the freedom to provide a broad range of financial services in all parts of the country. This transformed them into universal banks and important competitors to other institutions in the banking sector. However, for many of them this new business model proved to be unsustainable.

Throughout the 90s and the first decade of this century, savings banks followed an aggressive strategy of mortgage and consumer credit which left them highly exposed to the collapse of the property market. The financial crisis has had a significant impact on the Spanish economy. It brought about an abrupt end of the real estate boom and in its wake severe losses for all Spanish banks. But the savings banks had been most exposed to commercial real estate and were therefore most affected by the downturn. Losses mounted and many savings banks were de facto bankrupt. In spite of their recently acquired status of being private institutions, they were rescued with public funds and/or were forced to merge with commercial banks. Before the crisis there had been 45 independent savings banks, and within only 4 years, this number was reduced to 11. Nonperforming loans, which had been as low as 1 percent in 2007, soared to 10 percent on average and much more in certain savings banks.

Amid a rapid deterioration in asset quality in 2009, the Spanish government and the Bank of Spain started a deep restructuring and consolidation in the savings banks sector (Bailey and Peck 2013). This restructuring is being monitored by the Fund for Orderly Bank Restructuring. To foster the consolidation process, the Bank of Spain introduced the new Institutional System of Protection (SIP), which was born in 2009 as holdings of savings banks where the participating players transfer part of their economic and political power and share the business risks but they maintain their autonomy as a legal entity. The idea behind the SIP was that bad savings banks could be refloated by operating under the umbrella of a solid financial holding of good and bad savings banks, without bearing the costs associated to merger and acquisitions.

There are mainly two reasons for the crisis of the Spanish savings banks sector. One is the half-hearted privatization, which endowed the savings banks with the status of private corporations that were allowed and perhaps even expected to operate on a nationwide scale, but at the same time left local politicians in very powerful positions. When ownership and governance are not adjusted to each other, failure can easily be expected. The second and complementary is the demise of the regional principle in 1988. This allowed the savings banks to expand their branch network to other regions, and many of them made use of this opportunity. As a consequence, savings banks opened so many branches outside of their traditional intervention areas that the branch density in Spain became two times as high as the euro-area average. This growth intensified competition in the Spanish banking sector, put pressure on profitability and, as a reaction, induced several savings banks to engage in high-margin, high-risk lines of business, most notably commercial real estate lending. When the real estate bubble burst from the year 2008, the savings banks were in deep trouble.

Regarding the credit cooperatives, they are small institutions, in most cases firmly rooted in rural areas. They have always been of much less importance than savings banks. Their market share has never surpassed 10 percent. Also their growth during the boom years of the 1990s and the early years of the new century was less pronounced. With only minor transformations, they kept their former institutional features and their strong local roots. This enabled them to achieve equally stable earnings and profits for many years. Of course, the real estate crisis and the economic crisis in Spain also have had an adverse impact on the cooperative banks. But because of their conservative business model, at least so far, they have been less exposed to the crisis and retained relatively high repayment rates in their lending operations.

2.2.2 *Banks as Key Players in the Spanish Corporate Governance*

The close link between banks and the governance of nonfinancial firms dates back to the first stages in the process of industrialization in Spain. Thereinafter banks have had close relationships with nonfinancial companies, both through lending and through stock. Bank–industry relationships in Spain are the ones from the model of universal banking or mixed banking. The only exception to this framework was the Basic Law of 1962 that forced the specialization of the bank through the separation between commercial banks—focused on short-term commercial credit and industrial banks—specialized in the long term. This law, which aimed to solve the important problem of medium-term credit and promote new banks engaged in long-term investments, turned out to be inefficient and was eliminated in 1974, because new investment banks were mainly owned by major commercial banks. During these early years, the banking activity was closely linked to the country's industrial development (Torrero 1991; Sáez and Martín 2000). The causes of this close relationship are both economic and legal: The lack of private funds, the risk taking that economic development required, or the lack of a deep enough capital market to channel the financial flows required.

A second stage would extend from 1975 to mid-1980s, during which banks divested and concentrated in short-term financing. This reorientation was also caused by a number of financial and legal factors: 1970s crisis reduced dramatically the industrial profits and, therefore, the profitability of shares in nonfinancial firms. In addition, the liberalization of the financial system and the development of capital markets widened the scope of possibilities to both banks and firms. We have to notice the growing need to fund the State public deficit, which shifted investment from the private sector to the public one and increased the return on public debt. Likewise, the legal convergence with the European Union imposed tighter restrictions regarding bank and industry links.

In the late 1980s, the increases in the equity prices and the search for loyal customers in an environment of growing competition among banks resulted in more interest of banks in keeping shares of nonfinancial firms. This is consistent with Bergés and Sánchez del Villar (1991), who find a significant positive relationship between bank stock returns and the stock returns of the firms companies in which the bank had shares. Several empirical studies confirm the cyclical nature of the banking presence in the ownership of nonfinancial companies. Thus, Blanch et al. (1990) show that the proportion of shares of nonfinancial firms in the portfolios of banks grew during the 1970s but turned down during the 1980s until the lowest point in 1987, when this proportion began to grow again. Chuliá (1990) provides data on the banks stakes in nonfinancial firms during the period 1982–1988 in Spain, Germany, United States, Japan, United Kingdom, and Italy. Throughout this period, the share of Spanish banks was the highest after Japan. However, unlike other countries, this proportion decreased in Spain until 1987, when the minimum was reached. The decline in bank activity affected not only shareholdings but also bank lending (Aerts et al. 2013).

A new expansion process of the banking presence took place in the 1990s, so that between 1992 and 1998 the shares of nonfinancial firms held by credit institutions grew by 113 percent (Sáez and Martín 2000). However, this process runs in parallel with the expansion of the Spanish capital markets and thus, it did not lead to any unbalance between markets and institutions (García Cestona et al. 2005).

There are several factors to explain the consolidation of the relationship between banks and industrial firms: (1) bank participation was significant in some industries, such as real estate. Banks made efforts to get clients among house buyers and tried to take advantages of the increasing housing prices. Indeed, some of them owned real estate firms. Also, they were very active in leveraged industries (e.g., Energy and petroleum) and financial firms (e.g., Leasing and renting companies); (2) the debt capitalization of deposit institutions through participation in diverse sectors such as tourism, leisure, communication, and so forth; and (3) the process of financial globalization, in which bank intervention eases to invest in geographically distant markets.

It is worthwhile to note the different behaviors of savings banks and banks during the last decade of the 20th century. Although the proportion of equities in bank portfolios scarcely grew, savings banks doubled their importance, even exceeding the industrial portfolio of banks in 1998. This divergence is mainly due to the increased interest of banks to expand internationally, reducing its level of domestic investment and also, to the lower portfolio of savings banks at the beginning of the period and their interest on going out from their original geographic area.

Nowadays, there are some common points and some differences among institutions (Casasola et al. 2001; Crespí and García Cestona 2002). Commercial banks, savings banks, and credit cooperatives have in common that they do not usually own a too high percentage of shares in order not to internalize the costs of expropriating minority shareholders. In spite of being low, this percentage is high enough to enable banks to control the firms. Some differences among the different kinds of banks are shown in Table 2.1. We report the type of bank when a bank is the largest (or second largest) shareholder of a nonfinancial firm. As one can see, savings banks are more prone to own shares than their counterparts, either as first or second shareholders. Commercial banks and credit cooperatives do not show significant differences among them.

Nonetheless, because the three kinds of banks can compete under equal conditions in markets, hereinafter we will include all of them under the general term of *banks*. In Table 2.2, we report some descriptive data about the presence of banks in the corporate governance of nonfinancial firms. We would like to stress the growing proportion of firms with at least one bank as shareholder (it increases from 58.1 percent to 63.2 percent between 1999 and 2002). This increase is even higher when we exclude investment banks to focus only on commercial banks (38.3 percent vs. 48.5 percent). We can infer that almost half of the Spanish quoted firms have a commercial bank as reference shareholder. The proportion of representatives of banks at the boards of directors is quite stable and, jointly,

Table 2.1 Distribution of banks as main shareholders

Type of bank	1st shareholder	2nd shareholder
Commercial banks	30%	24%
Savings banks	39%	49%
Credit cooperatives	31%	27%
Total	100%	100%

Source: Casasola *et al*. (2001).

Notes: Percentage of each type of bank as largest (or second largest) shareholder of the nonfinancial firms whose largest (or second largest) shareholder is a bank.

two thirds of Spanish listed firms are somehow under banking influence, either as shareholder or as director.

In Table 2.3, we report some data about the characteristics of banks as shareholders. There has been an increase in the mean number of banks owning significant proportions of shares (1.6 banks vs. 2.3 banks), although the average stake of each bank remains with small changes.

In Table 2.4, we report some descriptive data about the firms with at least one director representing banks. Although the mean number of

Table 2.2 Banks as participants in the corporate governance

Bank role	1999	2002
Bank as shareholder	58.1%	63.2%
Shareholder and creditor	28.4%	32.3%
Shareholder but not creditor	19.7%	30.9%
Commercial bank as shareholder	38.3%	48.5%
Bank as director	38.3%	37.5%
Director and creditor	23.4%	19.8%
Director but not creditor	13.9%	17.7%
Shareholder and/or director	63.1%	68.4%

Source: Tejerina (2006).

Table 2.3 Banks as shareholders

	1999	2002
Average number of banks as shareholders per firm	1.6	2.3
Mean percentage of shares	19.6	21.1

Source: Tejerina (2006).

Table 2.4 Banks on the board of directors

	1999	2002
Average number of bank directors	2.3	2.5
Proportion of banking directors	20.1%	21.5%
Proportion of firms with unaffiliated directors	74.1%	80.4%
Proportion of firms with outside directors	46.3%	37.2%
Proportion of firms with banks as shareholders	87.0%	86.3%

Source: Tejerina (2006).

bank directors and the proportion on the whole board do not change significantly, there is a different trend conditional on the type of director: Although unaffiliated directors are more usual, the proportion of outside directors appointed by banks decreases. We will deal with the role of banks as shareholders and directors of nonfinancial firms in the next chapters.

2.2.3 The Spanish Stock Market

The Spanish securities market has undergone a deep process of change and growth over the last two decades. Technical, operating, and organization systems that support the market today have allowed important investment flows and provided the markets with greater transparency, liquidity, and efficiency.

Nowadays, Spanish stock market is highly concentrated with a relatively small number of players in the utility, telecommunications, banking, construction, and energy industries dominating the trading and capitalization. Following the massive privatization program of the 1990s, the introduction of electronic trading and the development of national and foreign investment funds, Spain's stock markets underwent a significant transformation and sustained growth for almost two decades.

Among the most important reforms has been the integration of the former four different stock markets (in Madrid, Barcelona, Bilbao, and Valencia) into a single holding company, *Bolsas y Mercados Españoles* (BME), with responsibility for trading, clearing, and settlement. The IBEX-35 is the benchmark stock market index of the Madrid Stock Exchange. Initiated in 1992, the index is managed and calculated by Sociedad de Bolsas, a subsidiary of BME. It is a market capitalization weighted index comprising the 35 most liquid Spanish stocks traded in the Madrid Stock Exchange General Index and it is reviewed twice a year.

One key landmark was the creation of the New Market in 2000, along the lines of US NASDAQ, in order to foster investment in highly technological firms. However, it lost momentum shortly after the dotcom crisis and closed just seven years later, in December 2007. One year later, a submarket was created, the Alternative Stock Market (MAB), aimed at highly innovative startups that need to raise funds in the market in order to grow. Although its importance is still very low (23 companies, which represent 0.12 percent of the Stock Market capitalization in 2013), the MAB has duplicated its capitalization since its creation in spite of the economic crisis.

In December 1999, Latibex was created. It is the only international market for Latin American securities. The market's creation was approved by the Spanish government and it is regulated by the Spanish Securities Market Law. It is based on the trading and settlement platform of the Spanish Stock Market, in such a way that Latin American securities listed on Latibex are traded and settled like any other Spanish security. It gives Latin American companies easy and efficient access to the European capital market. The number of firms listed in Latibex remains around 30 since its creation. Finally, an Open outcry trading is still used for a small group of less liquid stocks.

Table 2.5 shows the number of companies listed on Spanish Stock Exchange between 2006 and 2012. We can see a significant reduction from 2008, when the crisis began to hit Spanish economy seriously.

Also equities market capitalization went down significantly from 2008 (it reduced to half in two years). By sectors, we can observe in Table 2.6 that between 2006 and 2012, most sectors experienced a severe reduction in their capitalization, especially *basic materials, industry, and construction,* which had about a 61 percent drop. Nevertheless this is not surprising

Table 2.5 Companies listed on Spanish stock exchange

	2006	2007	2008	2009	2010	2011	2012
Electronic order book (SIBE)	139	166	141	133	129	130	127
Market for growth companies (MAB)	—	—	—	2	12	17	22
Latibex	34	34	33	32	29	29	27
Other companies (Outcry System)	52	42	39	37	35	34	31
Total	225	242	213	204	205	210	207

Source: Bolsas y Mercados Españoles (2014).
Note: Data includes SIBE, Outcry System, MAB, and Latibex.

because construction is the most affected sector by the real estate bubble. Only *technology and communications* withstood the first charge of the crisis but curiously it has dropped significantly in the last two years. What really attracts the attention is the behavior of *consumer goods*, which increase its capitalization by 55 percent during the same period.

With regard to capitalization by sector (Table 2.6 and Figure 2.5), the greatest contributions to the value of traded shares come from banks (largely as a result of capital increases and the rise in the share price of the two largest banks, which offset the fall in the share price of other banks) and former utilities firms that were privatized (energy and water, and transport and telecommunications). The value of the consumer goods industry is due to the sharp rise in the price of Inditex shares in recent years.

Finally, Table 2.7 shows the ranking capitalization in 2012 for the Spanish Stock Market. Apart from Inditex, S.A. (*consumer goods*) and Abertis Infraestructuras, S.A. (*basic materials, industry, and construction*) the most valued companies are banks (3), or they belong to *oil and energy* (4) and *technology and telecommunications* (1).

Table 2.6 Spanish equity market capitalization

	2006	2008	2010	2011	2012
Oil and energy	153,580	148,809	112,910	95,509	85,520
Basic materials, industry, and construction	96,204	44,471	46,480	40,803	37,000
Consumer goods	55,070	33,549	49,570	54,032	85,345
Consumer services	55,567	23,628	25,102	23,258	26,108
Financial and real estate services	281,243	150,095	150,263	138,075	146,514
Technology and telecommunications	83,854	77,785	87,009	68,687	56,955
MAB	23,705	24,648	26,922	24,373	24,607
Foreign equity	384,914	281,955	573,389	521,321	483,887
Total	1,134,137	784,942	1,071,633	966,058	945,935

Source: Bolsas y Mercados Españoles (2014).
Note: Data in million euros.

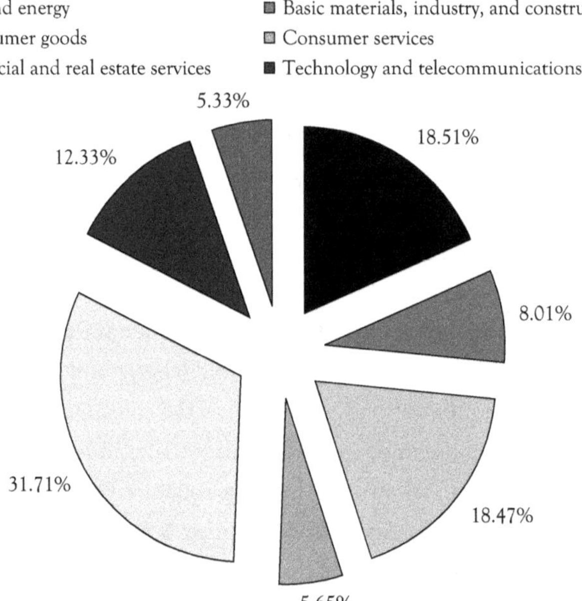

Figure 2.5 Distribution of market capitalization by industries

Source: Bolsas y Mercados Españoles (2014).
Note: Proportion of each industry in market capitalization (end of 2012).

Table 2.7 Capitalization ranking in 2012

Company	Value
Industria de Diseño y Textil, S.A. (INDITEX)	65,761
Banco Santander, S.A.	62,959
Telefonica, S.A.	46,374
Banco Bilbao Vizcaya Argentaria, S.A. (BBVA)	37,923
Iberdrola, S.A.	25,752
Repsol, S.A.	19,263
Endesa, S.A.	17,861
Gas Natural SDG, S.A.	13,589
Caixabank, S.A.	11,383
Abertis Infraestructuras, S.A.	10,119

Source: Bolsas y Mercados Españoles (2014).
Notes: Data in million euros. Largest Spanish companies by market capitalization.

2.3 The Legal Framework of the Spanish Corporate Governance

2.3.1 Spanish Companies Organization

Spanish companies have legal personality and thus can acquire rights and assets and assume liability. Companies must have their Articles of Association prescribing the terms and conditions for the functioning of the firm. These reflect the contract and relationship between shareholders and contain the rules for the company, including rules on shareholder meetings, powers and duties of directors, and many other aspects related to governance. In case of conflict, legal provisions normally prevail over Articles of Association (Cajigas García-Inés and López Muñoz 2013).

There are two main types of companies: public limited companies and private limited companies. In the public limited companies (*Sociedad Anónima* [S.A.]) shareholder liability is generally limited to the amounts contributed to the company's equity. This participation is represented by shares that qualify as negotiable securities, which may be listed on the stock markets. The minimum capital to set up an S.A. is 60,000 euro, which must be fully subscribed and at least 25 percent paid up upon incorporation. The issuance of nonvoting shares is also allowed. The holders of these nonvoting shares are entitled to receive minimum annual dividends, whether fixed or variable, as established in the company's articles of association according to the framework provided by the applicable law.

In the private limited companies (*Sociedad Limitada* [S.L.]), the partner liability is generally limited to the investment in the company's equity. The minimum capital required to set up an S.L. is 3,000 euro, which must be subscribed and fully paid up upon incorporation. The capital is represented by *quotas*, an instrument that closely resembles the shares of a public limited company, and which can also have a nonvoting nature. However, quotas may not be listed on stock markets.

Although public limited company used to be the most common form of company in Spain, private limited company has become more popular because of its flexibility in terms of incorporation (more economical), organization, and management. It is currently by far the most common type of business organization for nonlisted companies.

Spanish corporate law also foresees the so-called European Limited Company, which is a kind of supranational company recognized in the European legal framework and regulated by EU legislation. The legal framework of the European Limited Company is essentially to extend freedom of establishment within the territory of the EU enabling companies to operate in the EU under the same regulations, which are directly applicable in all member states. In this regard, member states are bound to adopt whatever measures are necessary to ensure the effectiveness of directly applicable EU rules. The model of European Limited Company is mainly aimed at large investments with a minimum called-up capital of 120,000 euro, although medium or even small companies are not excluded.

However, this kind of business is quite uncommon in Spain and in many other European countries (with the exception of Germany, where it has been sometimes used as a way to dilute employees' codetermination), because their regulation is somewhat impractical (e.g., there is a withdrawal right for shareholders who vote against a change of the company's registered office to another member country).

There are also three main types of partnerships in Spain, with a reduced presence in the Spanish business sector, due to the unlimited liability of their members (most of them). One of them can be the general partnerships, a private entity (*sociedad colectiva*) with legal personality and unlimited joint liability. There are also simple limited partnerships (*sociedad comanditaria*) and limited shareholders partnerships (*sociedad comanditaria por acciones*), both of which have legal personality and two types of partners: (1) general partners with unlimited liability; and (2) limited partners with limited liability up to their contribution.

Finally, there are also other types of business organizations or associations, which in most cases do not have a separate legal personality to that of their members. These entities include the following: temporary business association, joint account contracts (*cuentas en participación*), joint ownership (*comunidad de bienes*), and civil law partnerships (*sociedad civil*).

2.3.2 Spanish Corporate Governance Regulation

Spain has a civil law-based legal system. Court decisions are not a source of law but are of interpretative value. Also it is a member of the EU and as such follows the standards set out by EU directives and regulations. Structurally, Spain has adopted a federal system of governance comprised of 17 autonomous regions, which can govern certain areas independently, mainly relating to public services (education, health, and others). As to company law and corporate regulations, these are fundamentally established by the Spanish central government and thus are applicable throughout the country. The main corporate governance sources in Spain are the legislation, several codes of Good Governance, and the Articles of Association of each company.

Regarding legislation in Spain, the legal regulation of corporate governance has evolved in the last years in the context of a higher European legal harmonization. As Ruiz Mallorquí and Santana Martín (2009) suggest, the development of the Spanish stock markets would not have been possible without an appropriate regulatory framework. Spain has experienced significant legal and institutional changes in order to increase the transparency of the stock markets and the level of protection of minority shareholders. One of the first milestones was the creation of the *Comisión Nacional del Mercado de Valores* (Spanish Stock Exchange Commission [CNMV]) in 1988. The CNMV is the agency in charge of supervising and inspecting the Spanish Stock Markets and the activities of all the participants in those markets. It was created by the Securities Market Law, which instituted indepth reforms of this segment of the Spanish financial system.

As a general rule, all the supervision, control, and inspection of the Spanish Stock Exchange is carried out by the CNMV. In some specific areas, however (e.g., the public debt market), this responsibility is shared with the Bank of Spain. So, a wide range of institutions that were linked to the Spanish government have taken on a centralized configuration. Completing this structure, the old publicly appointed brokers (Stock and Exchange Agents) have lost their monopoly in equity trading. These were single-capacity intermediaries that could only act as agents on behalf of their clients or as principals on their own account, but who were always remunerated with statutorily fixed commissions. They were replaced by new corporate intermediaries who may act as both brokers and dealers (Securities Societies and Agencies).

The purpose of the CNMV is to ensure the transparency of the Spanish market and the correct formation of prices, and to protect investors. The CNMV promotes the disclosure of any information required to achieve these ends, by any means at its disposal. The CNMV focuses particularly on improving the quality of information disclosure to the market, and particular efforts are made in the area of auditing and in developing new disclosure requirements relating to remuneration schemes for directors and executives that are linked to the price of the shares of the company. Also, considerable efforts are made to detect and pursue illegal activities by unregistered intermediaries.

The actions of the CNMV relate to companies that issue securities for public placement, to the secondary markets in securities, and to investment services companies. The Commission also exercises prudential supervision in order to ensure transaction security and the solvency of the system. These entities are collective investment schemes (investment companies and mutual funds), dealers, and portfolio management companies.

The regulatory framework was updated in 1998 (Law 37/98) in order to introduce the requirements of the EU and favor the development of European Stock Markets.

Another significant yardstick in the Spanish corporate governance regulatory framework is the so-called Financial Law (Measures for the Improvement of the Financial System Act) in 2002. It was passed to increase the efficiency and competitiveness of Spanish financial markets and to strengthen investor protection. This law incorporated several EU Directives into Spanish law. According to this law, listed companies must have audit committees, formed by a majority of independent nonexecutive directors. This law also defines the relevant information that listed companies are required to disclose, and the rules of conduct for directors and employees of stock market–related entities regarding insider trading information.

In 2003, the Law on Transparency of Listed Companies was passed in order to reinforce transparency in public listed companies. This law creates new control mechanisms to increase security and transparency in the markets. It also introduces some amendments affecting the casting of votes and representation in the shareholders general meeting, and the shareholder's right to information, as well as the duties of diligence, faithfulness, and loyalty of directors, together with its liability regime. Additionally, the new law sets a series of obligations, such as adoption of rules of procedure for the board of directors, the director's conflict of interest and obligation not to vote at a shareholders general meeting when he or she has made a public request for representation if such conflict of interest exists. In the context of the new law, listed companies are required to submit to the CNMV an annual report on corporate governance and to disclose such information through a mandatory corporate website.

The Annual Corporate Governance Report that Spanish public listed companies have been filling since 2004 was intended to provide comprehensive and reasoned information on listed companies' corporate governance structures and practices. The CNMV is responsible for ensuring issuers' compliance, checking that the Report contains accurate data and adheres to all legal provisions. It is also empowered to request any information it deems necessary to monitor the implementation of corporate governance rules. Firms, thus, from 2004 onward have had to *explain* their Corporate Governance rules with a large degree of detail.

In spite of being a civil law country, the recently passed laws to improve the transparence of the Spanish capital markets have actually increased the level of protection of minority shareholders over the mean of the civil law countries. For example, La Porta et al. (1998) define an antidirector rights index to measure how the legal system provides effective protection to minority shareholders. Whereas the mean value for the civil law countries of such index is 2.33, Spain has a 4 points index. Similarly, Djankov et al. (2008) update this index and report that Spain achieves 5 points, whereas the mean of the countries similar to Spain is 2.91. Likewise, La Porta et al. (2006) assess the index of corporate information disclosure. Whereas the mean disclosure requirement in the French civil environment is 0.45, Spain has a 0.5 index. In the same vein, liability standard (an index of insider accountability) for Spain is 0.66, whereas the mean value for the French civil law countries is 0.39.

Nowadays, the primary corporate legislation is contained within the Company's Act Law (2010). The same year, Law 12/2010 introduced important reforms for the auditing profession, and to the stock market and corporate law based on the 1885 Commercial Law. This new law sought to comply with the EU harmonization policies and it entails, among other things, a substantive amendment to Spanish corporate law affecting listed corporations, namely, a prohibition on voting ceilings for shareholders, regardless of the number of shares they own. The amendment means Spanish law is closely aligned with some European countries such as Germany and Italy that prohibit voting ceilings in the bylaws of listed companies. In practice, the new law will make entrenchment tactics more difficult for listed corporations and therefore it facilitates takeovers and the entry of new investors in the ownership of publicly listed firms.

In general, the set of regulatory changes introduced in the last years foster efficiency in the securities, credit, and insurance markets; increase competitiveness in the financial sector; increase transparency and accountability; facilitate electronic trading; and strengthen the Spanish market for corporate control (Bailey and Peck 2013).

2.3.3 Soft Regulation

Apart from this legislation, corporate governance in Spain is also subject to soft rules through the development of several codes of good governance. The Spanish path on corporate governance started with the publication of a report by the Managers' Circle of Madrid (Círculo de Empresarios de Madrid), a Spanish association of businessmen, in 1996. The report showed a series of ideas and proposals for a better functioning of the board of directors.

The Spanish history regarding the codes of best practices, as in other Continental European countries, is relatively recent. The first official Code of Good Governance (the Olivencia Code) was issued in Spain in 1998. Since then, two other official Codes have been issued in Spain: The Aldama Report in 2003 and the Spanish Unified Code on Good Corporate Governance in 2006. Besides, private institutions and foundations have also issued Codes or initiatives in this direction: the Managers' Circle of Madrid in 1996 (*Circulo de Empresarios de Madrid*), the Foundation of Financial Analysis (*Fundacion de Estudios Financieros*), a foundation of the Spanish Association of Financial Analysts in 2002, and more recently the Institute of Directors (*Instituto de Consejeros*) and the Institute of Family Businesses (*Instituto de la Empresa Familiar*).

In February 1997, the Council of Ministers of Spanish government agreed on the development of a special commission to study an ethic code for the board of directors within companies. The purpose of the special commission was (1) to write a report about the board of directors of listed companies; and (2) to elaborate an ethic code of good governance, which listed companies could voluntarily follow. One year later, in February 1998, the first official Spanish Corporate Governance Code, the Olivencia Report, was published. Although the Committee recognized the special ownership structure of Spanish firms and made certain recommendations regarding the protection of minority shareholders, its recommendations were not far from the ones of the Cadbury Report.

One of its main objectives was guarantee transparency and better support for shareholders' interests. In particular, the report emphasized the following in the board of director's mission: General function supervision, core of nondelegable functions, and creation of value for the shareholders. The report finished with 23 recommendations. The recommendations dealt with the need to establish a majority of nonexecutive directors within the board, with the setting up of specialized committees made up exclusively of nonexecutive directors (i.e., the auditing, remuneration, and nomination committees) and with the need to disclose managers' and directors' pay deals and the need for directors' remuneration to depend on the firms' value. Recommendations calling for a maximum and minimum board size between five and 15 directors, respectively, and the setting of a retirement age for directors also figured in the Code. Given the institutional nature of Spanish companies, a hallmark of which is high shareholder concentration, the Code also established three types of directors: nonexecutives who are, or who represent, large shareholders, named nonexecutive owner or nominee directors, independent directors, and executive directors.

According to Ansón and García (2009) the success of the Olivencia Report was limited. The mean compliance with the Code recommendations in 2000 stood at 81 percent but only two firms out of 66 complied with all recommendations. For the year 2001, mean compliance was 77 percent, with only five firms implementing all 23 recommendations. The firms with a higher percentage of free-float, larger firms, and firms that had recently made public offerings were the ones that tended not only to comply to a greater extent with the Olivencia Report, but also to voluntarily provide the market with information on their compliance levels and corporate governance characteristics.

Some years later, the Council of Ministers approved the establishment of a special commission, fostering transparency and security in markets and listed companies, which published its report in January 2003 known as the Aldama Report. The Aldama Report followed the line of the Olivencia Code, essentially endorsing the philosophy of the rule of law, self-regulation of markets, and maximum transparency.

The Report introduced the concept of loyalty and diligence of managers and related to the functioning of the board of directors, and the shareholders' meeting. Given the institutional features of Spanish firms' ownership structure, the Aldama Report recommended that the composition of the board of directors should reflect the firms' ownership structure. It also recommended the establishment of Board committees and emphasized the importance of informational transparency. Actually, the core recommendation of the Aldama Report was that companies should be obliged to give fuller information about their systems of governance. This recommendation found an immediate echo in the Transparency Law, a Reform of the Spanish Company Law passed in July 2003.

Some of the recommendations of these two reports were introduced in Spanish legislation. The Law on Measures for the Improvement of the Financial System Act (2002) established that listed companies must have audit committees, formed by a majority of independent nonexecutives directors. Also it set relevant information on listed companies, and the rules of conduct for directors and employees of listed companies, in reference to insider trading information and the prohibition to distort the prices. A year later, the Law on Transparency of Listed Companies (2003) modified the Equity Market Law (1988), to reinforce transparency in public listed firms in the following terms:

1. Creates new control mechanisms to increase security and transparency in the markets.
2. Introduces some amendments to previous legislation applicable not only to listed companies, but to all, affecting the casting of votes and representation in the shareholders general meeting, and the shareholders' right to information, as well as the duties of diligence, faithfulness, and loyalty of directors, together with its liability regime.
3. Within the strict scope of the incorporated listed companies, established several obligations such as the adoption of rules of procedure

for the board of directors, the directors' conflict of interest and obligation not to vote at a shareholders general meeting, when he has made a public request for representation if such conflict of interest exists, and the establishment of a corporate governance annual report and information through a mandatory corporate website informing about it.

After the issuance of the Aldama Report, the Ministry of Economy called on CNMV to publish a single text with existing Corporate Governance recommendations, for listed companies to use as a benchmark when reporting their compliance or otherwise with corporate governance recommendations in their annual corporate governance reports. Subsequently, a Government agreement of July 29, 2005, ordered the creation of a Special Working Group to assist the CNMV, to unify the recommendations in place up to 2003, taking into account recommendations made after that date by different institutions, as the Principles of Corporate Governance, by the Organization for Economic Cooperation and Development (OECD), the European Commission recommendations, and the Recommendations on Corporate Governance for Banking Organizations approved by the Basel Committee on Banking Supervision. After several months of work, the Group completed its proceedings on May 2006, and unanimously approved the accompanying Report named "The Unified Code on Good Corporate Governance." Spanish listed companies must use the Unified Code as a reference when presenting their annual corporate governance reports from the information of year 2007 onward.

The Unified Code on Good Corporate Governance, as the Olivencia Code and the Aldama Report, is confined to companies whose shares are traded on the Stock Exchanges, and only to governance issues, not corporate social responsibility issues being the fulfillment of its recommendations voluntary. The new report covers 58 recommendations to fulfill, that can be segmented in board of directors, directors, and committee recommendations. It establishes recommendations on size and structure of the board of directors; publication of board remuneration in annual reports, directors' independence; publication of the companies' audited financial statements, in their public offering prospectuses when they issue securities, as well as in their listing ones when a security is admitted to trading on a regulated market. Overall, we can highlight some new subjects such as gender diversity in committees or higher transparency in remunerations.

One of its novelties is the use of binding definitions referring, among other matters, to the different groups of directors. A director can only be termed independent if he or she meets the minimum conditions that the Unified Code specifies that enable a person to perform their duties in a reasonable objective and independent manner. The principle of *complain or explain* is also easier to apply with the new Code as, previously, the coexistence of two codes made it more difficult to explain the compliance with their recommendations.

They are therefore failing to comply at an aggregate level with 11.1 percent of recommendations (13 percent in 2010). The largest and the most traded companies (i.e., the ones in the IBEX-35 index) present a degree of noncompliance (4 percent on average) considerably below that of remaining firms.

Under the *comply or explain* principle, companies must state their degree of compliance with the Code's 58 recommendations, indicating whether they comply with them fully, partially or not at all, giving reasons, as the case may be, for any practices or criteria departing from the same. Figure 2.6

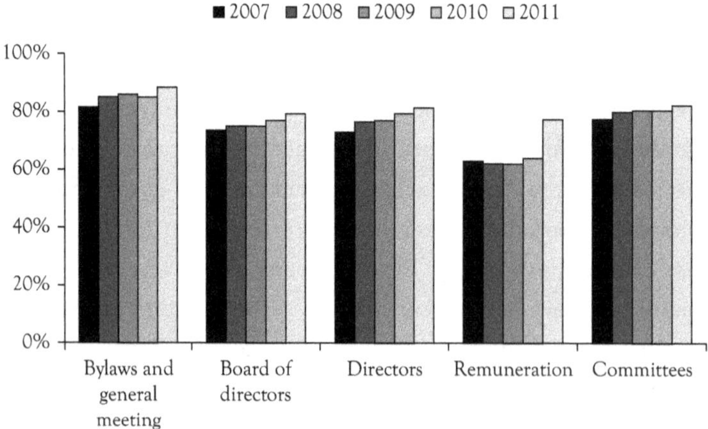

Figure 2.6 Degree of compliance with unified code recommendations

Source: CNMV (2011).

shows companies' total average compliance with Unified Code recommendations in each category in the years 2007–2011.

Overall, compliance with Code recommendations rose along the years analyzed. Improvement was most marked in recommendations dealing with the approval and transparency of director's remuneration. Listed companies comply on average with 81.3 percent of the Code's recommendations and partially with a further 7.6 percent. The advance in compliance is in part a consequence of the implementation in national law of two recommendations, those referring the obligation of the board to submit a report on directors' remuneration policy to the general meeting and the one that forces that this report must detail individual compensation. Companies are therefore failing to comply at aggregate level with 11.1 percent of recommendations. The largest and the most traded companies (i.e., the ones in the IBEX-35 index) present a degree of noncompliance (4 percent on average) considerably below that of remaining firms.

They are therefore failing to comply at aggregate level with 11.1 percent of recommendations (13 percent in 2010). The largest and the most traded companies (i.e., the ones in the IBEX-35 index) present a degree of noncompliance (4 percent on average) considerably below that of remaining firms.

In April 2013, Spanish Council of Ministers approved the submission of the 2013 Reform Program and the 2013–2016 Spain Stability Program update to the EU and the European Commission. Both documents reflect Spain's economic policy strategy for the coming years. One of the points in the National Reform Program is the reform of corporate governance. The aim is to reform and expand the current framework of corporate governance best practices in Spain in order to enhance efficiency and accountability in the management of Spanish companies and, at the same time, to set the bar for Spanish standards at the highest level of compliance. To do so the next measures are envisaged:

1. Preparing an analysis of international corporate governance best practices and the areas in which Spain can improve its current framework with a view to implementing appropriate reforms in the near future.

2. Strengthen the role of shareholders' meetings in monitoring the compensation arrangements for managing bodies and senior executives. In addition, the recommendations of the Spanish Unified Code of Best Practices for unlisted Spanish companies will be expanded and the possibility of preparing a Code of Best Practice for unlisted companies will be analyzed and new improvements introduced into the governance of credit institutions in line with legal developments in the EU.

CHAPTER 3

Internal Mechanisms of Corporate Governance in Spain

3.1 The Board of Directors

Board of directors is one of the most analyzed internal mechanisms in the literature to the extent of being referred as the apex of the internal control system. This assertion is especially relevant because the very purpose of the internal control mechanism is to provide an early warning system to put the organization back on track before difficulties reach a crisis stage. Formal economic theorizing about boards has been quite limited. But, to some extent, the vacuum in formal theory has been filled by empirical work on boards. A number of empirical regularities have been established by the empirical literature. First, some characteristics of board such as the composition are not always correlated with firm performance. Second, board actions seem to be related to board characteristics. Finally, boards appear to evolve over time depending on the bargaining position of the CEO relative to that of existing directors.

In Spain, firms are managed and represented by the management body, which may adopt different forms, such as (1) a sole director, (2) various members acting jointly and severally, and (3) a board of directors. In Private Limited Companies, the articles of association may establish different ways of organizing the firm's management, such as granting the shareholders' meeting, the ability to choose any form between those foreseen without modifying the articles of the association. In these firms, the number of the management body will not exceed 12. Regarding Public Limited Companies, Spanish law provides for a standard one-tier board structure. Actually, listed firms must have a board of directors. Only European Limited Companies (with an insignificant number in Spain) may choose a two-tier board, where directors assume the management of the company and a supervisory body controls their performance.

3.1.1 *Legal Regulation*

The main functions that the members of the Board of Directors should assume are: (1) to approve the firm's strategy and the necessary media to follow it; and (2) to monitor and control how the executives and officers achieve the detailed target and observe the corporate purpose and the company's interests.

There are also some specific positions with specific functions. In this way, the Chairman, besides dealing with calling the board, establishing the agenda, and conducting the meetings, will also ensure that the members of the Board receive necessary information enabling them to participate in the debates and the decision-making process. The Secretary of the board must facilitate the running of the meetings and take care to supply directors the information they need in advance. The Secretary must also keep minutes of the Board meetings and certify resolutions. In addition, the Secretary will ensure that the proceedings and acts of the Board of Directors comply with the legal and material form contained within its own rules of corporate governance.

Spanish legislation emphasizes two general duties: To act diligently and to be loyal to the interests of the firm. These duties are instrumented through several specific obligations:

- Diligent management: Directors will carry out their tasks with the diligence of a prudent business person and must diligently be informed concerning the running of the business of the firm.
- Loyalty: All directors have duty of loyalty. They must act in the best interest of the company and comply with the duties established in the articles of association and the applicable laws and regulations.
- Prohibition of using the firm's name or referring to his or her condition as director of the company in order to perform acts for himself or herself or for related parties.

- Prohibition to take advantage of business opportunities regarding investments or activities affecting the firm's assets when that investment was known by the member of the company as a consequence of his or her condition as such, or the firm having interest on it.
- Duty to notify conflicts of interest: Members of the Board of Directors must notify remaining members—or in case of a sole director the Shareholders' Meeting—of any direct or indirect conflictive situation that might arise and cause damage in relation to the interests of the firm. Members must inform of such situation as well as of any relationship that they or any related parties may have with competitors in the market; they must also communicate the tasks or faculties performed in those companies. Such information must be published in the Annual Report.
- Prohibition of competition: Unless previously authorized by the firm, directors may not carry out, whether in his or her own name or on behalf of a third party, activities that are identical or similar to those of the company's corporate purpose.
- Secrecy: Members of the Board of Directors, even after the cessation of their positions, must keep duty of secrecy in relation to confidential information known due to their position, unless legal provisions authorized them to do so.

Directors will be liable before the company, shareholders, and the firm's creditors, for any damage caused as a result of willful or negligent acts or omissions contrary to the law or the articles of association or in breach of their duties. Furthermore, the Board of Directors and management can incur in personal liability (civil, administrative, or even criminal) for the actions of the company under certain circumstances such as failing to pay social security contributions, breaches of health and safety at work regulations, and so on.

The Unified Code states that the board's mission should be the definition of the company's general strategy, the control of its day-to-day management and communication with its shareholders. For these objectives to be met, the boards' size should be aligned with the particular needs of each issuer, and its membership should pursue a sufficient diversity of knowledge, gender, and experience for it to perform its functions efficiently, objectively, and in an independent way. From this approach, we are going to show the main variables that describe the average board of directors in Spain.

There is no prohibition regarding the nature of the members. Therefore, either an individual or a company may become directors. A director is not required to be a shareholder and need neither be a resident in Spain nor be a Spanish national. Directors are ordinarily appointed by the Shareholders' Meeting. However, in the case of Public Limited Companies, Spanish law allows shareholders to form groups and appoint a number of members of the board in proportion to the percentage of ownership that each group holds. Also, Spanish regulation foresees coopting appointments. In these cases, the Board of Directors may appoint a shareholder as a director to cover an unforeseen vacancy or when no substitute director has been appointed, until the next Shareholders' Meeting takes place. The directors of a Public Limited Company are appointed for a period of time stated in the articles of the firm, which may not exceed six years. Directors of Private Limited Companies can be appointed for an indefinite term, unless the articles state otherwise. However, in both cases, directors can be reelected for the same period of time, again unless the articles of the association provide otherwise.

The Code of Corporate Governance recommends that the proposal for the appointment and renewal of members that the Board submits to the Shareholders' Meeting should be approved by the Board of Directors on the proposal of the Nomination Committee (in the case of independent directors) or subject to a report from the Nomination Committee in other cases.

3.1.2 The Size of the Board

Size is one of the more studied variables related with the board of directors. Mínguez and Martín Ugedo (2005) find an inverse relationship between the firm value and the size of its board in Spain. On the contrary, Fernández et al. (1998) showed a nonlinear relationship between firm value and board size. At the beginning, the increase in board size leads

Table 3.1 The evolution of the board size in Spain

2004		2006		2008		2010	
IBEX-35	Continuous market	IBEX-35	Continuous market	IBEX-35	Continuous market	IBEX-35	Continuous market
14.9	10.9	14.6	10.8	14.5	10.9	14.4	11.2

Source: Fundación de Estudios Financieros (2011).

to more firm value until there comes a time when that relationship reverses. These authors suggest that in a certain moment the problems of coordination overcome the advantages attached to a greater board.

The Code of Corporate Governance of Listed Companies establishes the ideal size for the Board of Directors between 5 and 15 members, in the interest of maximum effectiveness and participation. The size of Spanish boards is to a great extent determined by the firm size. Beyond this fact, board size remains stable along the last decade. The bigger the firm, the bigger the board of directors. Table 3.1 shows the number of directors in different years according with the *Corporate Governance Observer Report* from the *Fundación de Estudios Financieros*. IBEX-35 encompasses the 35 most traded companies, that is, it is made up by big firms. The Continuous Market, with near 140 firms, includes also medium and even small firms. We can see that the number of directors stays stable and it is bigger among the IBEX-35 firms.

Also in the previous years, the number of directors did not undergo substantial variations. Stuart reported a number of directors between 12 and 13 in the period 1997–2002 for a sample of 80 to 90 firms. More recently, PricewaterhouseCoopers placed the number of directors for a 50 companies sample between 13 and 14 from 2009 to 2013. These numbers get close to the maximum recommendation number of directors in the Unified Code (15).

Figure 3.1 shows the average size of listed companies boards of directors over 2008–2011, grouped according to market capitalization. We can confirm that the biggest companies have the biggest boards.

Table 3.2 tracks the changing size of listed company board, grouped once more by market capitalization. It should be noted that 85.2 percent of companies reported board sizes within the minimum of five maximum

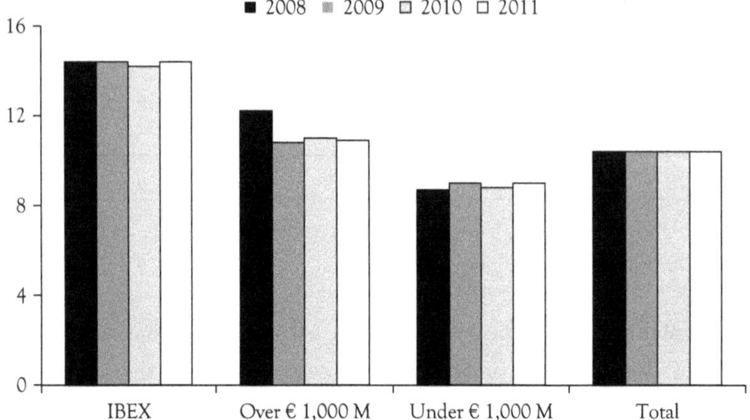

Figure 3.1 Average board size

Source: CNMV (2011).

of 15 members urged by the Unified Code. As in previous years, overshoots were mainly among the IBEX-35 group, with 11 companies reporting more than 15 members. Boards of fewer than five members were mainly among companies capitalizing at under 1,000 million euros.

3.1.3 The Composition of the Board

As in the international sphere, the conclusions about the relationship between board composition and firm performance in Spain are ambiguous. Fernández et al. (1998) find a significant and positive relationship between firm value and nonexecutive directors. These authors also show that a higher external director ratio has a greater influence in top management rotation. However, that link is not found by Gispert (1998), who finds a negative and significant relationship between firm performance and directors rotation, although such relationship is not strengthened by nonexecutive directors. In addition, Mínguez and Martín Ugedo (2005) show a negative relationship between directors' ownership and external directors' percentage, suggesting that both of them are substitute governance mechanisms. Nevertheless, Leech and Manjón (2002) conclude that when ownership concentration is high, as it is in Spain, some governance mechanisms such as the board of directors and institutional shareholders

Table 3.2 Distribution of companies according to board size

	Under 5 members				Between 5 and 10 members				Between 11 and 15 members				Over 15 members			
	2008	2009	2010	2011	2008	2009	2010	2011	2008	2009	2010	2011	2008	2009	2010	2011
IBEX-35	0	0	0	0	7	6	5	5	16	17	19	19	12	11	11	11
Over € 1,000 M	0	0	0	0	5	6	7	6	8	7	6	3	2	1	1	1
Under € 1,000M	9	7	6	5	73	70	71	68	28	27	23	26	4	4	4	5
TOTAL	**9**	**7**	**6**	**5**	**85**	**82**	**83**	**79**	**52**	**51**	**48**	**48**	**18**	**16**	**16**	**17**
%	**5.5**	**4.5**	**3.9**	**3.4**	**51.8**	**52.6**	**54.2**	**53.0**	**31.7**	**32.7**	**31.4**	**32.2**	**11**	**10.3**	**10.5**	**11.4**

Source: CNMV (2011).

Note: Number of firms conditional on the size of the board.

do not play a very significant role in corporate governance. Finally, Andrés et al. (2010) found that the quality of the directors, in particular if they are bankers, is a relevant variable to take into account in the relationship between board characteristics and firm value.

The Unified Code draws a distinction between internal directors (executive) and external directors (owners, independent, and others). When an external director cannot be classed as either owner or independent, the company should explain the circumstances in their Corporate Governance report.

Regarding board composition, Table 3.3 shows its evolution throughout the period 1997–2002 for a panel of 80 to 90 firms. It is very noted the significant growth in the percentage of independent directors between 1997 and 1998 (just when the Olivencia Code was published). This growth goes hand by hand with the decrease in executive directors and, more significantly, in owner directors.

Using a different and more recent sample (Table 3.4), we also find a high stability pattern. The table also shows that in the samples with smaller firms, there are more executives and owner directors, but less independent ones. This makes sense because small and medium firms use to have more concentrated ownership and lesser ownership-control separation.

The Unified Code recommends a balance between external and internal directors. It also recommends that the ratio of owner directors to independents should reflect the relationship in the company's capital between nominating shareholders and the rest. Figure 3.2 charts the relationship between both types of directors over the last four years. The four

Table 3.3 Board composition (I)

	1997	1998	1999	2000	2001	2002
Executives	27	23	25	19	19	19
Owners	52	37	37	42	44	44
Independents	21	40	38	39	37	37
Total (%)	100	100	100	100	100	100

Source: Spencer Stuart (2002).
Note: Percentage of directors by type.

Table 3.4 Board composition (II)

Board composition	2006		2008		2010		2012
Sample	IBEX-35	Continuous market	IBEX-35	Continuous market	IBEX-35	Continuous market	IBEX-35 + 16 firms
% Executives	19.7	19.9	17.7	19.2	17.2	19.1	17
% Owners	36.5	43.6	38.2	43.4	36.8	43.0	40
% Independents	39.9	33.5	38.5	32.4	41.4	33.3	39
% Others	3.8	3.1	5.5	4.9	4.6	4.6	4

Sources: Fundación de Estudios Financieros (2011) and PricewaterhouseCoopers (2013).

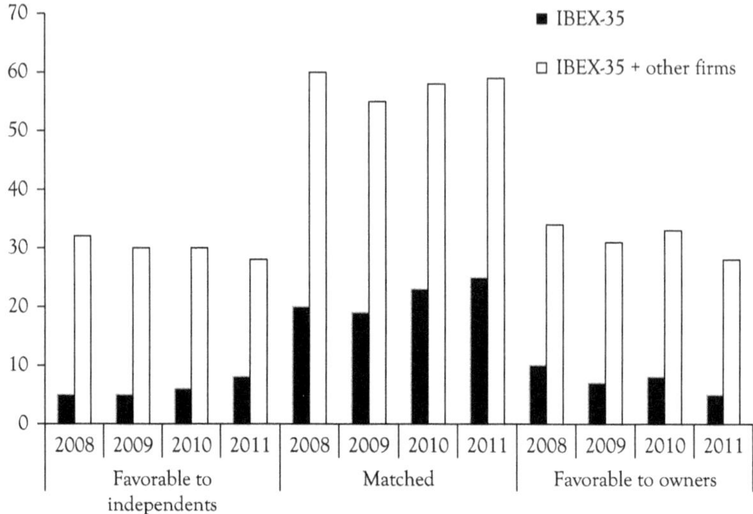

Figure 3.2 Balance between owners and independent directors

Source: CNMV (2011).
Note: Number of firms according to the prevalence of independent vs. owner directors.

left side columns are the firms in which independent directors are overrepresented relative to shareholders, whereas the four right hand columns are the number of firms in whose board shareholders are overrepresented. It can be seen as a trend toward a balanced board in which the proportion of independent and owner directors is in accordance with the composition of the capital. Specifically, in the last four years, the percentage of companies reporting a balanced mix has risen by 5.9 points—11.4 points among IBEX-35 members—as far as 77.9 percent of the total sample (82.9 percent of the IBEX-35 group).

Independent directors are those in a position to perform their duties without being influenced by ties with the company, its significant shareholders, or its management team. Instead, they are appointed to the board on the strength of their personal and professional qualities. The Unified Code recommends that independent directors should occupy, at least a third of board places. As we can observe in Table 3.5, overall independents' board representation falls short of the one thirds recommended.

The one-point improvement in independents' board representation traced mainly to the increase reported among companies with market

Table 3.5 ***Presence of independent directors on boards***

	Less than 1/3 board members				Between 1/3 and 50% of board members				Over 50% of board members			
	2008	**2009**	**2010**	**2011**	**2008**	**2009**	**2010**	**2011**	**2008**	**2009**	**2010**	**2011**
IBEX	10	8	10	9	19	19	19	16	6	7	6	10
Over € 1,000 M	12	9	8	8	3	5	5	1			1	1
Under € 1,000 M	67	69	58	51	35	37	37	45	12	11	9	8
Total	89	86	76	68	57	52	61	62	18	18	16	19
%	54.3	55.1	49.7	45.6	34.7	33.3	39.9	41.6	11.0	11.5	10.5	12.8

Source: CNMV (2011).

Note: Number of firms according to the proportion of independent directors.

capitalization below 1,000 million euros. Nevertheless, the number of firms reporting no independents on their boards dropped to 10.1 percent. The number of companies incorporating a 12-year limit on independents' board tenure, as recommended by the Unified Code, has risen from 37 in 2008 to 44 in 2011.

3.1.4 *Board Committees*

Listed firms in Spain usually have, in addition to a managing director holding delegated powers from the Board, an Executive Committee with similar powers that in practice operates as a reduced board. In some firms, the function of the executive committee is to hold meetings in a more regular way than the Board of Directors. The Code of Corporate Governance of Listed Companies recommends, however, that the Board was kept fully informed of the discussions and decisions adopted by the executive committee.

In addition, Boards of listed companies must have a compulsory Audit Committee, formed by members of the board (a majority of whom must be external ones) and, as a recommendation of the Code of Corporate Governance of Listed Companies, chaired by an independent director. At least one of its members must have accounting or auditing knowledge. The role of the Audit Committee is mainly of an advisory nature and refers to the supervision of auditing practices, the relationship with the external and internal auditors, paying special attention to the independence of external auditors, the control of risk management policies and the review of the financial information that the firm has to make public.

Also, the Code of Corporate Governance of Listed Companies recommends the creation of a nomination or remuneration committee (or both). This committee should be made up mostly by independent directors and chaired by one of them. The nomination and remuneration committee have advisory powers in matters such as the selection of candidates for the board, the right to make proposals (or inform of the proposals made by the board) relating to the appointment of directors and the right to propose (or inform the proposal by the board) remunerations policies.

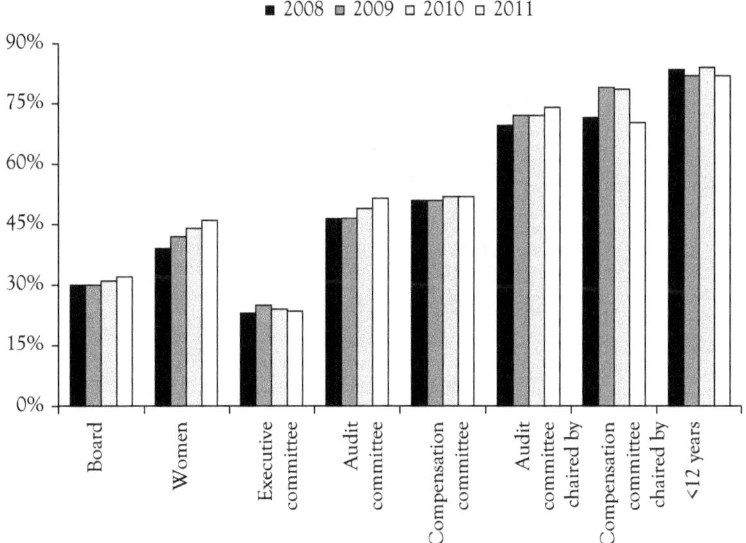

Figure 3.3 Presence of independent directors

Source: CNMV (2011).

Notes: Proportion of independent directors in the board and in the most usual committees. We also report the proportion of committees chaired by independent directions and the proportion of directors having been nominated less than 12 years ago.

Figure 3.3 tracks the progress of the main variables indicating the relative weight of independent directors on the governing bodies of listed companies. Executive committees featured the lowest percentage of independents (24.1 percent), whereas in the audit committee and in the nomination and remuneration one, the percentage of independent directors approximate to 50 percent. Only 4 percent of directors occupying the chair belong to the independent category, with only six companies (among 149) in this situation. In the case of the vice chair position, the proportion of independent incumbents rises to 22.6 percent.

Table 3.6 shows the percentage of firms with a particular committee. Beyond the Audit committee (compulsory by law), we observe that the Nomination and Remuneration committee is nowadays in almost all the companies. Likewise, Executive committee is much more common in the samples with a bigger median firm size. Finally, Strategy and Risks committees are the ones less used.

Table 3.6 Percentage of firms with committees

	2004		2007		2010		2012
	IBEX-35	Continuous market	IBEX-35	Continuous market	IBEX-35	Continuous market	IBEX-35 + 16 firms
Audit	100	100	100	100	100	100	100
Executive	85.3	46.3	83	46	79.5	45	66
Nomination and remuneration	100	90	97	81	100	95	100
Strategy	6	8	9	10	14.7	13.7	18
Risks					10		12

Sources: Fundación de Estudios Financieros (2011) and PricewaterhouseCoopers (2013).

Next, we analyze the main committees deeply. The breadth of the powers that the laws and by-laws confer on listed company boards counsels the creation of board committees to carry out delegated executive functions. Corporate governance principles urge maximum transparency in the relationships between the board of directors and executive committees. In particular, their composition should match that of the board, because otherwise they may exercise their delegated powers from a divergent perspective. In this sense, we can see from Figure 3.4 that executive directors have occupied a higher share of executive committee versus board places in each of the last four years. We can also see that, as last year, the directors classed as other external were the only ones equally represented on both bodies.

Regarding audit committee, the Code recommends that it should be made up exclusively of external directors, and chaired by an independent. In an annual Corporate Governance Report (including 149 firms), *Comisión Nacional del Mercado de Valores* (CNMV) states that audit committees have an average of 3.6 members. Among IBEX-35 firms, the average stands at 4.1 members. Figure 3.5 charts the weight of different director categories in listed company audit committees. The audit committees of 81.6 percent of listed companies are made up of 100 percent of external directors, with 48.3 having a majority of independents. Of this group, 18 companies have an audit committee formed entirely of independent directors.

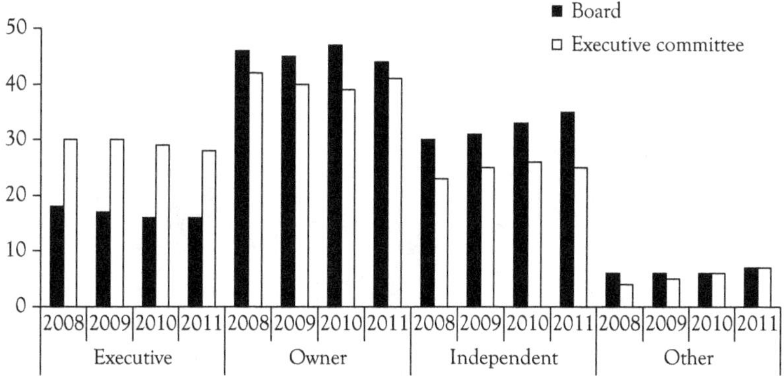

Figure 3.4 Types of directors on the executive committee and on the board

Source: CNMV (2011).

The Unified Code describes the function of the nomination and remuneration committee as follows: to oversee the integrity of the selection process for company directors and top executives, ensuring that candidates meet the target profile for each vacancy; to advise and organize the handover of the company's chair and chief executive positions; to report to the board on matters of gender diversity, among others.

It also advocates that this committee be formed entirely of external directors, the majority independent, under the chairmanship of an independent, and that it should propose the candidates for independent directorships as well as issuing a report on all other prospective appointees. The average members of the nomination and remuneration committee is 3.7. All IBEX-35 companies operate this committee. Figure 3.6 shows

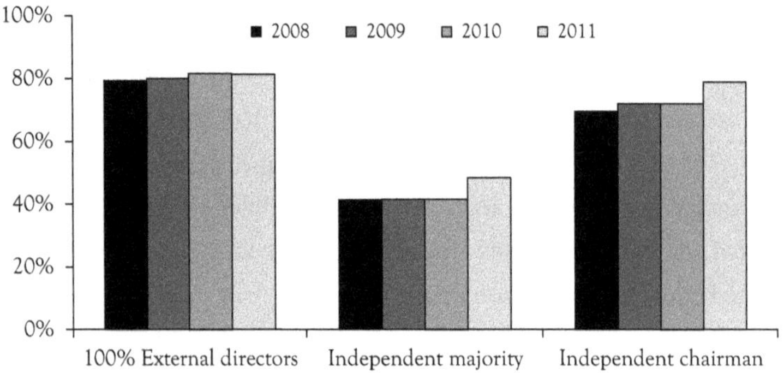

Figure 3.5 Audit committee membership

Source: CNMV (2011).

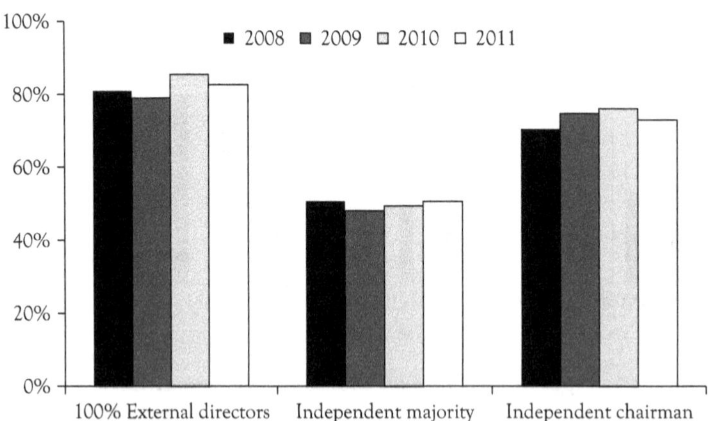

Figure 3.6 Nomination and remuneration committee membership

Source: CNMV (2011).

the weight of different director categories in listed company nomination and remuneration committees. 42.9 percent of the companies follow the Unified Code recommendations on nomination committee membership. Independents are in a majority at 69 companies and in 16 of them make up 100 percent of the committee's places.

3.1.5 *Board Shareholdings*

The average equity stake held by the board of directors is 28.3 percent. Figure 3.7 gives the average distribution of board shareholdings with companies grouped by market capitalization. We can observe that board shareholding is inversely related to the size of the company. Directors of firms under 1,000 million euros of capitalization hold approximately 35 percent of firms' shares.

By type of director, Figure 3.8 shows the distribution of capital by director category; 75.7 percent of executive directors hold equity stakes in their employer companies. Of this percentage, 4 percent declared holdings of over 50 percent, and a further 12.7 percent declared holdings of between 10 percent and 50 percent. Regarding owner directors, 61.5 percent of them own shares in listed companies, 49.3 percent reporting shares of more than 3 percent of capital. Finally, 58.4 percent of independent directors report holding shares in listed companies. Nevertheless, of these directors, 80.3 percent have an ownership stake below 0.1 percent.

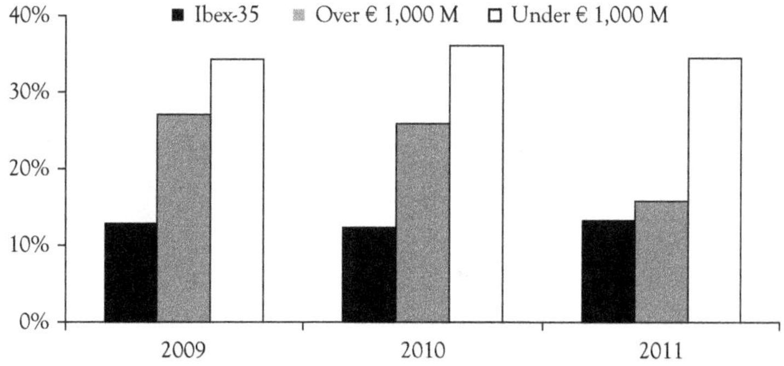

Figure 3.7 Distribution of board shareholdings

Source: CNMV (2011).

Note: Proportion of shares owned by the directors according to the size of the firm (measured by market capitalization).

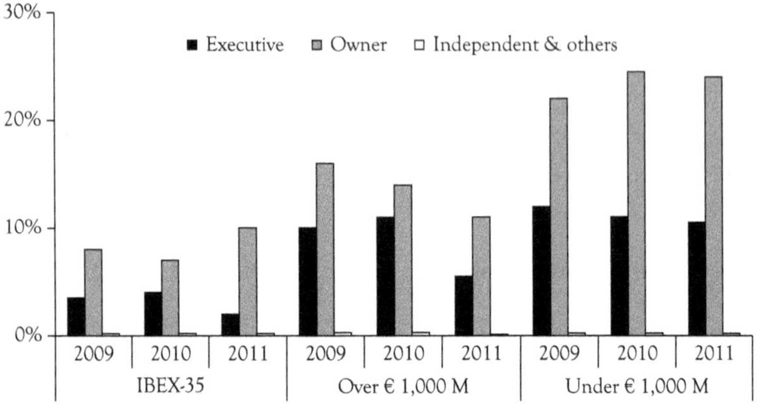

Figure 3.8 Distribution of capital by director category

Source: CNMV (2011).

3.1.6 Board Compensation

World Economic Forum (2014) is among the first to provide empirical evidence on the relationship between board remuneration and the performance of the large Spanish companies. The Sustainable Economy Law (2011) requires public limited companies to prepare an annual report on the remuneration of directors. This report must set out full, clear, and comprehensible information on the company's remuneration policy, as approved by the board for the current year, and, where applicable, remuneration policy for future years and a global summary of how the policy has been applied in the year just ended, with a breakdown of the individual remuneration accruing to each director.

Aside from the obligation to draw up an annual report on directors' remuneration, companies must supply aggregate information on board pay in their Annual Corporate Governance Reports. Firms should detail certain remuneration items such as nonvariable remuneration, variable payments, expenses, directors' fees, share-based compensation, and other benefits, as well as quantifying the total accruing in the company and its group with a breakdown by director category.

Figure 3.9 tracks the average compensation of the whole board in listed companies. We also report the aggregated compensation of executive directors and external directors over the 2004–2010 period.

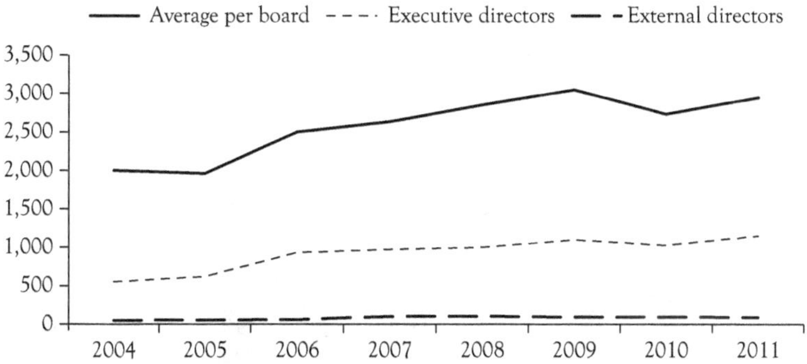

Figure 3.9 Board member remuneration

Source: CNMV (2011).
Note: Average compensation of the whole set of directors. Data in thousands of euros.

Average remuneration per board in 2011 stood at 2.9 million euros, the highest levels in the previous decade; 14.5 percent of companies reported a remuneration increase exceeding 20 percent. At 11 percent, the increase ranged from 10 percent to 20 percent, whereas a further 20.7 percent reported increases of below 10 percent. Conversely, 44.1 percent of listed companies said their board remuneration was lower than the year before. Also it is significant that executive directors are much better remunerated than external directors.

Figure 3.10 sets out board remuneration by item. We can see that the variable component, excluding share-based compensation, has gained ground in 2011, whereas nonperformance-related pay (fixed remuneration, expenses, and fees) has moved down 2.3 percentage points.

Fixed remuneration is the nonvariable monetary compensation paid to directors with a set periodicity for the work they do on the board, regardless of their attendance at board meetings, and, in the case of executive directors, for carrying out their duties as senior managers. Figure 3.11 shows the percentage of annual change per board of the fixed remuneration.

Variable remuneration is reserved in most cases for executive directors, and includes monetary amounts linked to the achievement of individual or group objectives and commensurate with other compensation or any other reference in euros. Its percentage annual change per board

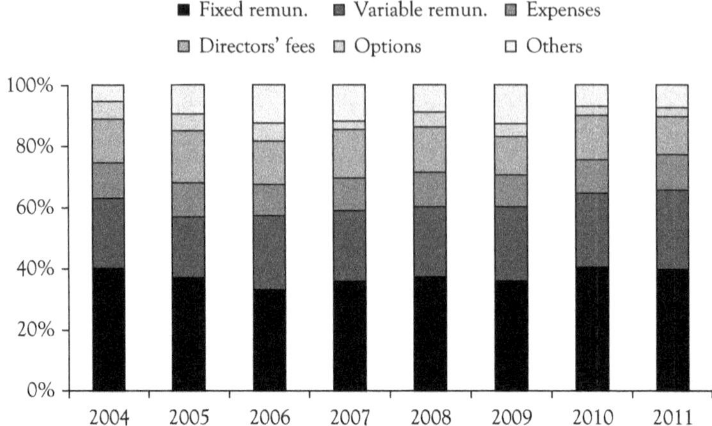

Figure 3.10 Composition of board compensation

Source: CNMV (2011).
Note: Percentage of each item on the whole compensation of the board.

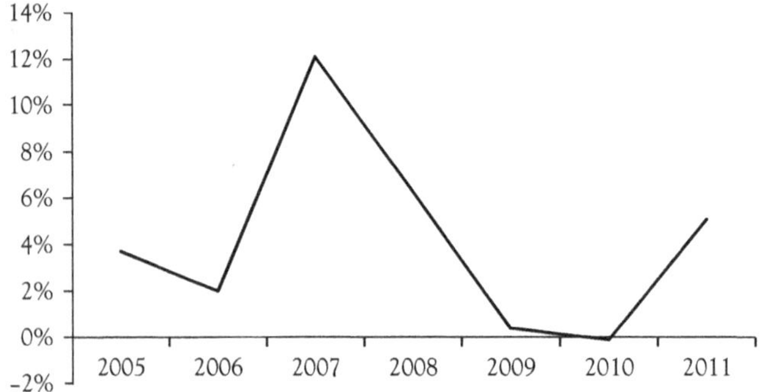

Figure 3.11 Annual change of the board fixed compensation

Source: CNMV (2011).

is showed in Figure 3.12. As we can see, the percent annual changes are more abrupt than the ones of fixed remuneration.

The expenses comprise payments in respect of directors' membership of governing bodies. Some firms pay a given amount for attendance at each meeting of the board or board committee, whereas others set a fixed sum for each body the directors serve on, regardless of how often it actually meets. Figure 3.13 shows its annual change over the reference period.

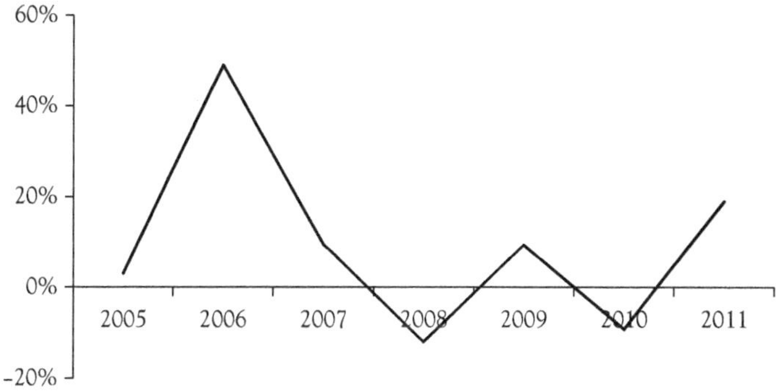

Figure 3.12 Annual change of the board variable compensation

Source: CNMV (2011).

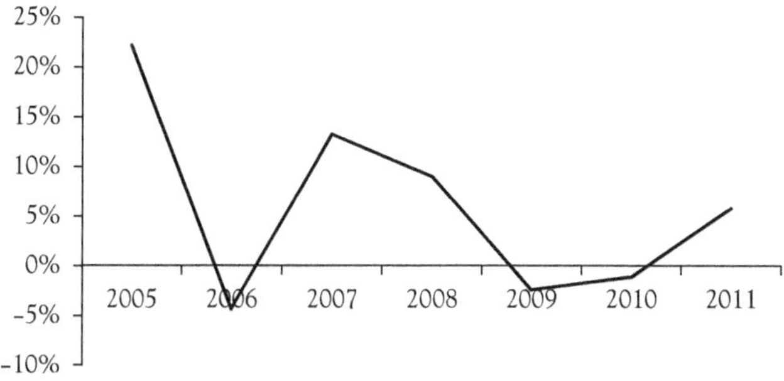

Figure 3.13 Annual change of the board expenses

Source: CNMV (2011).

Regarding directors' fees, these are annual amounts payable to all board members regardless of which category they belong to, whose annual change evolution in the 2005–2011 period is shown in Figure 3.14.

Share options and similar remuneration packages mainly benefit executive directors. Share options tend to be packaged into medium- and long-term incentive schemes to secure the loyalty of senior management. Figure 3.15 tracks its percentage annual change.

Finally, other remuneration category includes severance payments; multiannual incentive schemes, which companies do not class as variable remuneration; and payments in kind. Severance payments are the weightiest items as well as the main determinant of year-on-year changes, given

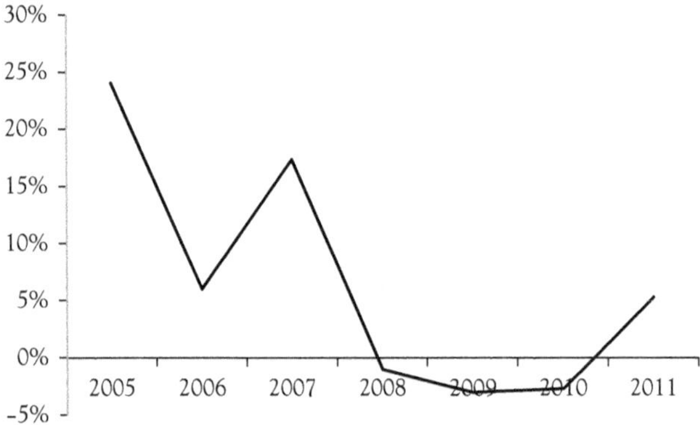

Figure 3.14 Annual change of the board fees

Source: CNMV (2011).

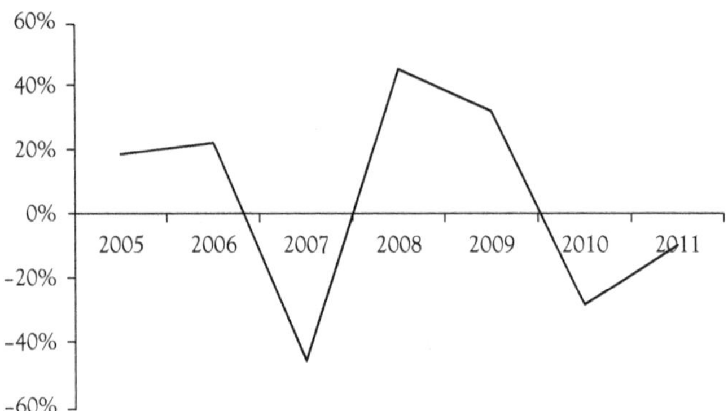

Figure 3.15 Annual change of the board stock options and similar

Source: CNMV (2011).

their volatile nature compared with previous kinds of board compensation (Figure 3.16).

3.1.7 Other Board Issues: Gender Diversity, Multiple Directorships, and Meetings

The Unified Code considers that a good gender balance on boards of directors is not just an ethical–political or corporate social responsibility issue; it is also an efficiency objective that listed companies should consider working toward. It accordingly urges companies with few or no women on their boards to deliberately cast round for female candidates

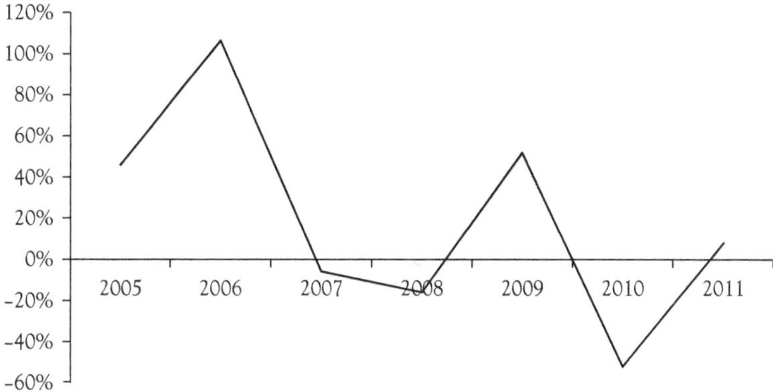

Figure 3.16 Annual change of the board compensation on other items

Source: CNMV (2011).

Figure 3.17 Percentage of women directors out of total board members

Source: CNMV (2011).

whenever a director position falls vacant. In this sense, Figure 3.17 charts the progression of female board membership and the split according to director type from 2008 to 2011.

The percentage of women board members has risen by 2.3 points since 2008, as far as 10.4 percent at 2011. In the independent category, women raised their share by 3.2 points to 14.9 percent in the same v. Conversely, their representation in the other external director category dropped to 7 percent in 2011, whereas their share of executive and owner director places is almost unchanged. Table 3.7 shows the number of board places

Table 3.7 Presence of women on boards

	No. of women directors				% Total				No. of companies with women directors				% Total			
	2008	2009	2010	2011	2008	2009	2010	2011	2008	2009	2010	2011	2008	2009	2010	2011
IBEX-35	44	50	53	60	8.7	10.2	10.6	11.9	26	27	29	31	74.3	79.4	82.9	88.6
Over € 1,000 M	12	13	17	11	6.6	8.4	10.9	9.9	7	6	9	7	46.7	42.9	64.3	70.0
Under € 1,000 M	82	87	88	91	7.1	8.8	9.4	9.6	55	58	60	61	48.2	53.7	57.7	58.7
Total	**138**	**150**	**158**	**162**	**8.1**	**9.2**	**9.9**	**10.4**	**88**	**91**	**98**	**99**	**53.7**	**58.3**	**64.1**	**66.4**

Source: CNMV (2011).

Note: Proportion of women on the board of the IBEX-35 firms, and of the large versus small quoted firms according to market capitalization.

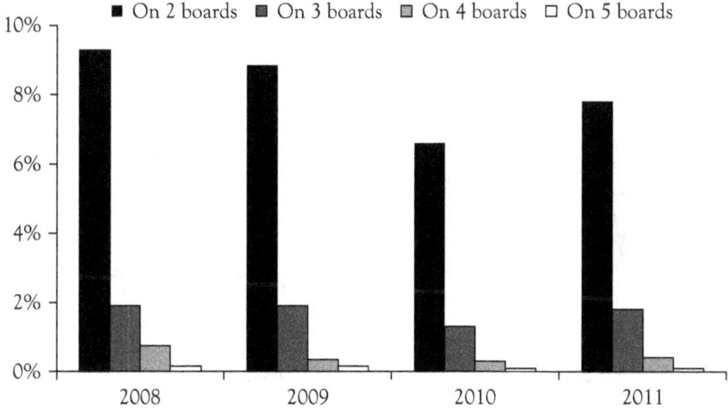

Figure 3.18 Percentage of directors belonging to more than one board

Source: CNMV (2011).

occupied by women during 2008 to 2011, together with the number of companies reporting female directors.

In 2011, 66.4 percent of listed companies had at least one woman on their boards. Within the IBEX-35 group, the percentage increases to 88.6 percent. Although the average percentage of women on boards has increased by 2.3 points in the last four years, the number of boards with women on them has increased by 12.7 points.

As far as multiple directorships are concerned, Figure 3.18 shows the percentage of board members holding directorships on more than one board. In 2011, a total of 1,381 persons occupied the 1,562 director posts at listed companies, giving a ratio of 1.13 directorships per head. A total of 1,241 directors (89.9 percent) held only one board place with the following breakdown by category: 17.8 percent executive, 43.8 percent owner, 31.7 percent independent, and 6.7 percent other external directors. Furthermore, 7.8 percent of directors sit on the boards of two companies, 1.8 percent on the boards of three and 0.4 percent on the boards of four. The proportion of directors sitting on over five listed companies is 0.1 percent.

As for board meetings, for the last 10 years the number of board's meeting remains between 10 and 11 per year. It is noted that when the median size of the sample is smaller, the number of meetings tends to be slightly lower.

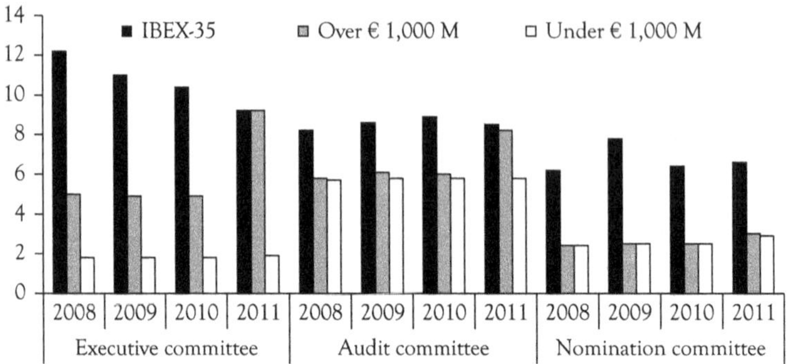

Figure 3.19 Average number of meetings by committees

Source: CNMV (2011).

Note: Average number of meetings by committees of the IBEX-35 firms, and of the large versus small quoted firms according to market capitalization.

Finally, Figure 3.19 shows the average number of meetings held by board committees in the past four years depending on the firms' capitalization. In general, more committee meetings occur in the biggest firms. By category, executive committee is the one with more meetings, followed by the audit committee and the nomination and remuneration committee.

3.2 The Ownership Structure of Spanish Listed Firms

In the previous decades, ownership structure has been one of the most analyzed corporate governance mechanisms (Meca and Ballesta 2009). Literature has shown that the nature of governance problems differs greatly between public companies with and without a controlling shareholder. With a controlling shareholder, the main governance problem is not anymore the opportunism by managers at the expense of shareholders but rather the opportunism by the controlling shareholder at the expense of the minority shareholders.

Investors with large ownership stakes have strong incentives to maximize their firm's value and are able to collect information and oversee managers, thus, they can overcome the traditional principal-agents' problem, the conflicts of interests between shareholders and managers. They also have enough voting control to put pressure on the management in some cases, or perhaps even to oust the management through a proxy fight or a takeover (Shleifer and Vishny 1986). So, they have both the interest in getting their money back and the power to demand it. However, the concentrated ownership structures also show a variety of costs. The most obvious is that large investors are not diversified, and hence bear excessive risk (Demsetz and Lehn 1985). Although this could be a problem for individual investors, it is not a difficulty for institutional investors. A more significant problem is that the large investors represent their own interests, which need not coincide with the interests of other investors in the firm, or with the interests of employees and managers (Shleifer and Vishny 1997). In the process of using his control rights to maximize his own welfare, the large investor can therefore redistribute wealth, in an efficient or inefficient way, from others. This cost becomes particularly important when other stakeholders have their own specific investments to make, which are distorted because of possible expropriation by the large investors.

3.2.1 *Ownership Structure: A Broad View*

Unlike models of widely dispersed corporate ownership, recent studies show that in most countries publicly traded firms often have large controlling shareholders, even in developed countries. La Porta et al. (2000b) traced the control chains of a sample of 30 firms in each of 27 countries. They document whether the firm has an ultimate controlling owner or, in the other case, it is a widely held one. Considering a 10 percent cutoff, they found that only 15 percent of Spanish large publicly traded firms are widely held (Zero percent in a medium-sized sample). So, clearly Spain can be included among the countries with a concentrated ownership.

As a bank-oriented economy, Spanish Stock Market is not as developed as its Anglo-Saxon counterparts. Table 3.8 sets out the aggregate amount of companies' equity book value and market capitalization in the years 2008–2011. The aggregate sum of market capitalization was down 10.2 percent with respect to 2010. The decline among IBEX-35 members was 8.8 percent. By far the biggest drop, 35.5 percent, was among companies with market capitalization exceeding 1,000 million euros. Among those with market capitalization between 500 and 1,000 million euros, the reduction came to 3.6 percent.

Table 3.8 Equity book value and market capitalization of listed companies

					Book value				Market capitalization			
	Number of companies				Million €				Million €			
Sector	2008	2009	2010	2011	2008	2009	2010	2011	2008	2009	2010	2011
Nonfinancial	141	134	132	127	26,768	25,793	29,060	26,222	340,439	351,070	320,951	284,256
Financial	23	22	21	22	10,906	11,067	11,468	16,431	134,457	192,686	141,923	131,388
Total	164	156	153	149	37,674	36,860	40,528	42,653	474,896	543,756	462,874	415,644
Size												
IBEX-35	35	34	35	35	29,944	29,797	30,681	33,323	400,910	485,820	413,015	376,576
Over € 1,000 M	15	14	14	10	2,289	1,167	3,640	2,783	47,500	31,004	28,167	18,161
Under € 1,000 M	114	108	104	104	5,441	5,896	6,207	6,546	26,486	26,932	21,693	20,907

Source: CNMV (2011).

Note: Equity book value and market capitalization of listed companies by sector and size (the breaking point is 1,000 million euros capitalization). Data in million euros.

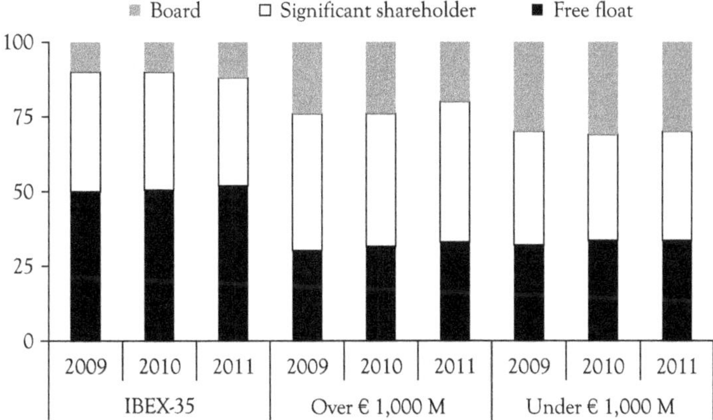

Figure 3.20 Distribution of capital by market capitalization group

Source: CNMV (2011).

The overall distribution of capital by type of shareholder has remained essentially unchanged in the previous years. We can see in Figure 3.20 that nondirector significant shareholders control approximately 32.5 percent, the board of directors' ownership is approximately 28.3 percent and free float rise the 37.5 percent. The rest is treasury stock, only 1.7 percent.

Table 3.9 provides additional evidence on the ownership concentration figures taken from the last report available from the Spanish Corporate Governance Observatory (Fundación de Estudios Financieros 2011). We can see that concentration remains in significantly high levels. It has slightly grown among IBEX-35 and high-capitalization firms in the previous years, whereas in medium- and low-capitalization firms ownership concentration has been reduced in the same period. Nevertheless, we can conclude that both the large and the three large shareholders ownership remain steady with time. These figures are consistent with different studies carried out in recent years for Spanish firms (Crespí and García Cestona 2002).

In Table 3.10, we report the number of companies according to the ownership share of significant shareholders. Out of the 23 listed companies whose nondirector significant shareholders have stakes of less than 5 percent, half of them are under the control of the board of directors.

Table 3.9 Ownership concentration by size

	Large shareholder %		3 Large shareholders %	
	2004–2008	2009	2004–2008	2009
IBEX-35	31.3	34.2	44.4	45.2
High capitalization	47.6	49.0	59.5	63.1
Medium capitalization	38.1	34.8	51.6	50.4
Low capitalization	29.2	28.4	44.0	45.4
Total sample (124 firms)	36.6	35.4	49.9	49.8

Source: Fundación de Estudios Financieros (2011).
Notes: No IBEX-35 firms are classified as follows: High capitalization firms (more than 1,000 million euros); medium capitalization firms (between 250 and 1,000 million euros); and low capitalization firms (less than 250 million euros).

3.2.2 Shareholders' Meeting

One area of corporate governance where international organizations like the OECD and the European Commission have been calling most strongly for improvement since the start of the crisis is the involvement of shareholders in general, and institutional investors in particular, in the life of listed companies.

This goal has also been addressed in Spain, where companies have been taking steps to encourage shareholders to exercise their attendance and voting rights. The amended text of the Corporate Enterprises Law has also brought novelties in this respect. Public listed companies, for instance, must now operate a website where they publish all materials relative to the organization and conduct of general meetings sufficiently in advance, along with the resolution adopted. The website must include an electronic shareholders' forum to facilitate shareholder communication in the lead-up to the meeting. Through this forum, shareholders can propose motions to be tabled, request support for such motions, or try to mobilize a sufficient percentage of votes to exercise a minority right. The Unified Code also devotes a chapter to the general meeting, including recommendations to the powers of the meeting, advance information on proposals, separate voting on separate items and the possibility of split votes.

Table 3.10 **Number of companies according to the stake of the significant shareholders**

	Under 5%				Between 5%–25%				Between 25%–50%				Over 50%			
	2008	2009	2010	2011	2008	2009	2010	2011	2008	2009	2010	2011	2008	2009	2010	2011
IBEX	4	6	4	5	9	9	11	11	8	7	5	8	14	12	15	11
Over € 1,000 M	2	2	2	0	3	2	3	2	4	3	3	3	6	7	6	5
Under € 1,000 M	22	24	19	18	34	29	39	38	28	29	22	24	30	26	24	24
TOTAL	**28**	**32**	**25**	**23**	**46**	**40**	**53**	**51**	**40**	**39**	**30**	**35**	**50**	**45**	**45**	**40**

Source: CNMV (2011).

Note: Companies are classified into IBEX-35 firms, firms with market capitalization over 1,000 million euros, and firms with market capitalization under 1,000 million euros.

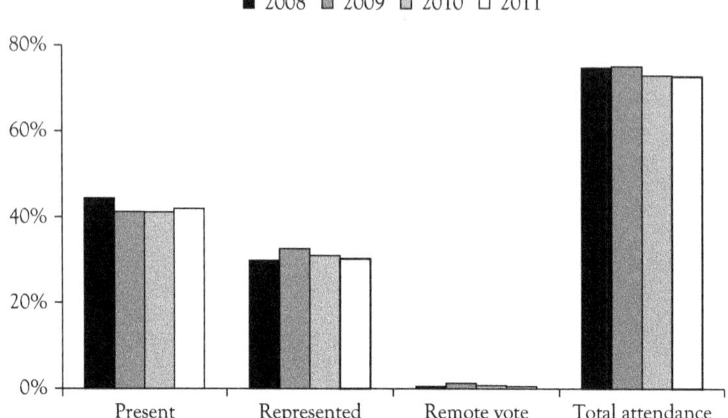

Figure 3.21 Participation in general shareholders meetings (I)

Source: CNMV (2011).

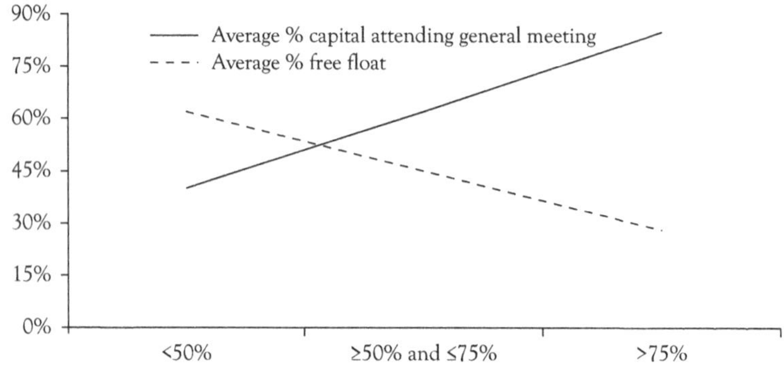

Figure 3.22 Participation in general shareholders meetings (II)

Source: CNMV (2011).

Figure 3.21 shows the average participation in the general meeting of listed companies between 2008 and 2011, indicating the percentages of capital present, represented and voting remotely. The average attendance at general meetings held in 2011 equated to 73 percent of share capital. Of the three participation conduits, physical attendance was the only one to register an increase, from 41.8 percent to 42.3 percent in a break with the trend prevailing since 2008.

Listed companies have been stepping up their efforts to get minority shareholders to participate in general meetings. The Figure 3.22 sets average attendance against free-floating capital for three participation intervals with reference to meetings held in 2011. It shows that a higher percentage of minorities tends to reduce general meetings attendance, which is favored, conversely, by a lower percentage of free float.

In addition, according to the Corporate Governance Report (Azofra Palenzuela 2012), 51 percent of the companies analyzed specify a minimum number of shares for attendance at their general meetings, normally under 1,500 shares. Nevertheless, the number of companies imposing an ownership threshold for attendance headed steadily lower between 2008 and 2011.

3.2.3 Large Shareholder Identity

One of the dimensions of ownership structure that has a significant influence on corporate governance is the nature of the main shareholder. The study of the identity of the large shareholder is specifically interesting with concentrated ownership structures, because not all types of investors have the same incentives and ability to exercise control. Potential owners differ in terms of wealth, costs of capital, competence, preferences for on-the-job consumption, and nonownership ties to the firm. These differences affect the way they exercise their ownership rights and therefore have important consequences for firm behavior and performance. In addition, potential investors can be affected in different ways by the laws and regulations in a particular country or financial system. Finally, economic literature suggests that agency costs associated with controlling minority shareholder structures depend on the identity of the large shareholder.

In Table 3.11, we present the evolution of the share ownership of Spanish listed companies in the last 20 years. From this table, we can infer several stylized facts. One of the most significant is the strong drop of the Spanish government as shareholder of public firms in 10 years (between 1992 and 2002) due to the privatization process that took place in the mid-1990s. This process meant the sale of stocks from the government to minor individual investors, institutional investors, and nonresidents in a first stage, and to nonfinancial firms mainly from 1997.

The picture that emerges from the analysis of the ownership structure with the latest available data is shown in Figure 3.23. An important

Table 3.11 Share ownership of Spanish listed companies

	1992	1997	2002	2007	2012
Banks	15.6	12.9	7.1	9.4	5.2
Insurance co.	3.4	2.6	2.2	2.2	3.0
Other institutional investors	1.7	7.6	5.2	6.0	5.4
Government	16.6	5.6	0.4	0.2	0.5
Nonfinancial firms	7.7	5.9	22.0	25.4	21.7
Families	24.4	30.0	28.3	20.1	25.1
Nonresidents	30.6	35.6	34.8	36.8	39.2

Source: Bolsas y Mercados Españoles (2013).
Note: Percentage of market capitalization held by the different types of shareholders.

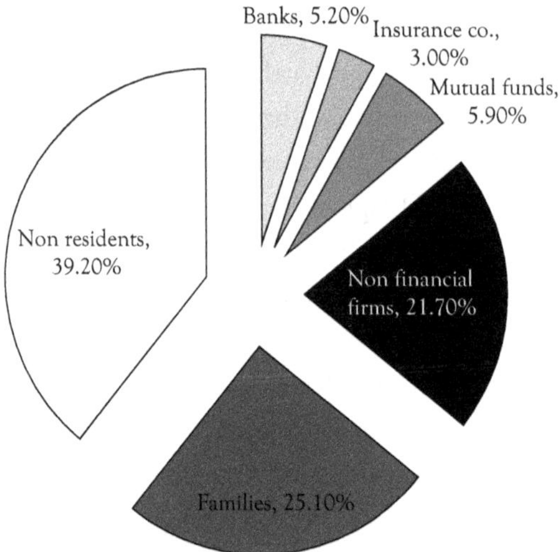

Figure 3.23 Distribution of capital by market capitalization group

Source: Bolsas y Mercados Españoles (2013).
Note: Percentage of market capitalization held by different types of shareholders.

category of shareholder, which after some ups and downs remains in a high level are families. Approximately 25 percent of listed companies' shares are in their hands. Families usually are very much involved in the management of the firms they control. In economic terms, they invest in firm-specific human capital, which creates long-term ties to the firm, that may or not be a source of value creation. Unlike other types of shareholders, families act on their own behalf and not as indirect representatives for other principles. This leads to a positive incentive alignment effect of family ownership. Moreover, family loyalty may overcome incentive problems and increase efficiency. But other factors, such as the ability to avoid a hostile takeover could imply a negative entrenchment effect if the family's share ownership exceeds a certain level. Furthermore, because families usually invest a large share of their wealth in the company, family-owned firms may be relatively risk averse, and they are more likely to be capital rationed. Succession problems and family conflicts may also damage family business. Actually, Burkhart et al. (2003) do not hesitate to attribute the prevalence of family firms to a weak investor protection financial system as the Spanish one is considered.

Regarding nonfinancial firms, they have multiplied their participation by three (from 7.7 percent in 1992 to 21.7 percent 20 years later). In addition, most nonresident shareholders (whose participation is very significant) are also nonfinancial firms. Sometimes nonfinancial firms hold shares in other companies as part of cross-ownership or company group structures. In these cases, ownership can facilitate access to valuable technology and other specific resources that can improve the value of their affiliated companies. Vertical ties between companies at different stages of the value chain make economic sense under conditions of high asset specificity and transaction frequency. In business groups, the ownership ties may be motivated by diversification of risk. Corporate owners are typically large and therefore may have better access to capital from both internal and external sources than family owners. Finally, business groups may have size-related advantages in political rent seeking.

As far as institutional investors are concerned, we have distinguished between banks (including savings banks) and other institutional investors because of the importance of the bank ties in the Spanish financial system. In general, financial institutions are assumed to be portfolio investors whose main objective is shareholder value. Nevertheless, there are exceptions to this rule: For example, banks may value the security of their loans and other business relations with the firm as much as their ownership interest. Pension funds may have links to trade unions or governments that make them sensitive to political concerns such as job safety or public image of the companies they invest in. However, holding a large portfolio of shares at arm's length distance and being evaluated regularly on their financial results will arguably make financial institutions strongly concerned with shareholder value. Compared with other ownership categories, they seem less likely to be wealth-constrained or to impose wealth-constraints on the firms that they own. Furthermore, financial investors are generally subjected to special regulation and supervision by government and, therefore, have relatively little scope for expropriation of wealth at the expense of minority shareholder.

From Table 3.11, we can see that banks ownership percentages in Spanish listed companies have reduced in a near steady way going from 15.6 percent in 1992 to 5.2 percent in 2012. Without doubt, financial crisis led many banks to get rid of some of their investments. Meanwhile, the participation of insurance companies remained stable along the previous 20 years and other institutional investors increase theirs, but staying at very low levels.

3.2.4 *Controlling Minority Shareholders*

Large controlling shareholders frequently own substantially more control rights than cash flow rights, making them what the literature terms as controlling minority shareholders (CMSs). These types of shareholders can entrench themselves against pressure from corporate governance mechanisms such as the market for corporate control or monitoring by noncontrolling shareholders. As a consequence, CMSs have the power to expropriate other shareholders, and this power is limited only by legal restrictions and by their own financial incentives not to engage in opportunistic behavior. Taking into account that expropriation is costly, rational CMSs face a tradeoff between value-enhancing activities and further extraction of private benefits of control, when maximizing their total utility. Because CMS internalizes only a minority fraction of negative corporate valuation consequences, but enjoys all of the private benefits, this tradeoff is in favor of private benefits extraction. Hence, the agency costs of CMSs are increasing the larger potential for private benefits extraction.

Basically there are three methods to achieve control rights in excess of cash flow rights: Dual-class shares, cross-holdings among firms, and pyramid structures. The last is the one most used in Spanish economy. Pyramiding occurs when the controlling shareholder owns one corporation through another, which he does not totally own. Firm F is held through *multiple control chains* if it has an ultimate owner who controls it via a multitude of control chains, each of which includes at least 5 percent of the voting rights at each link. This kind of structure has been documented mainly in Western Europe and Asia (Claessens et al. 2002; Faccio and Lang 2002; Cronqvist and Nilsson 2003).

Table 3.12 shows control shareholder identity figures coming from two different studies of Spanish listed firms using control chains. In both studies, the cutoff point to identify any shareholder as a significant one is 10 percent. We observe that more than a half of the companies are controlled by families. This percentage is higher in the Faccio and Lang's study due to them considering a greater number of firms in the sample, so including smaller ones, among who family control is more frequent. From the table it is also possible to highlight the relevant widely controlled financial firms.

Table 3.12 Distribution of the largest shareholder identity

	Faccio and Lang	**Santana and Aguiar**	
	1997	**1999**	**2002**
Families	74.07	50.0	52.2
Widely held nonfinancial firms	1.69	9.4	8.1
Widely held financial firms	11.11	21.9	24.3
State ownership	3.61	3.1	1.8
Others	0.47	2.1	1.8
Disperse ownership (<10%)	9.06	13.5	11.7
Total no. of firms	**530**	**96**	**111**

Sources: Faccio and Lang (2002) and Santana and Aguiar (2006).
Note: Percentage of firms according to the identity of the largest shareholder

Table 3.13 Right differences depending on the largest shareholder identity

	Control rights	Cash flow rights	Rights difference
Families	46.40	36.19	10.21
Banks	31.94	25.85	6.09
Widely held nonfinancial firms	61.21	61.16	0.05
Other institutional investors	41.18	38.39	2.79
State	53.14	46.48	6.66
Others	12.98	12.98	0

Source: Tejerina (2006).

Average difference between control (voting) rights and cash flow rights depending on the identity of the largest shareholder.

Regarding the differences between control and cash flow rights among Spanish firms, Table 3.13 reports, for a 136 firm sample, the percentage of both types of rights of the large shareholder (Tejerina 2006). As we can see, families is the category with greater difference, followed by banks. Hence, according to the literature, they are the most susceptible type of control shareholder to behave in an opportunistic way.

3.2.5 The Role of Banks

Although in the recent years the role of banks in the governance of nonfinancial firms has decreased, it is still very significant. The bank–industry relationships have been traditionally very tight in Spanish economy. In a bank-oriented financial system, banks are the most important providers of external finance, in particular for small and medium-size firms. So the banks' role in the financing and governance of firms is relevant for the smooth functioning and growth of an economy. Banks do not only interact with firms through debt financing, but they also play an important role as shareholders and board members.

Firms and banks enter into a relationship to overcome problems of asymmetric information. Without such a relationship, firms may be financially constrained. The existence of financial intermediation may be the reduction in the cost of monitoring information and therefore the resolution of incentive problems in the debt markets. Banks screen firms' loan applications, and monitor firms by designing loan contracts and by interacting frequently. Also, bank loans signal the credit worthiness of firms to other market players, and thereby reduce the information costs for the other contracts. Nevertheless, when banks get private information about firms, they may use it to extract rents in the future. This problem is known as the *hold-up problem* in banking literature and may be in part overcome through the bank participation in the ownership.

Schneider-Lenné (1992) points to three reasons for a bank to become a shareholder of a nonfinancial firm: (1) as a way to protect its investment when the company is in a difficult financial situation; (2) as a financial investment that allows the bank to protect its profits and reduce risk through asset diversification; and (3) as a method to enhance bank relations. Banks can be interested in keeping relationships with its customers under a system of reciprocal benefits, according to which, in the economic upturns the company provides the bank with a profitable and safe business segment, and in the economic downturns the firms benefit from the bank support. By acting as a shareholder or as a director, banks manage to keep stable relationships with firms.

However, owning shares of nonfinancial firms can be costly and risky for banks. First, it can lead to excessive risk concentration in case banks are simultaneously lender and shareholder. Second, there are costs as a result of the exit barriers—both economic and social ones—that prevent banks from leaving smoothly the firm or force banks to lend excessive amounts of money. In addition, the publication of news on bad results of companies owned by banks can result in distrust and concern in capital markets. Fourth, equity is riskier than other financial investments and this leads to riskier bank portfolios. Finally, keeping a portfolio of nonfinancial firms requires a highly trained team to provide support to the owned companies.

In addition to owning shares, financial institutions can keep ties with nonfinancial firms by being involved in the boards of directors. Although research on the presence of bank directors is less frequent than the analysis of bank ownership participation, some studies have shed some light on this issue. As shown by Dittmann et al. (2010), the benefits of the presence of a bank director can be summarized in informational terms.

First, it improves the flow of information between the bank and the company because a completely comprehensive debt contract would be extremely unlikely and prohibitively expensive. Literature has traditionally underlined the function of external expertise provision (Li and Harrison 2008; Lehn et al. 2009). By being directors, banks act as firms' advisors with a broad experience with different companies, sectors, and managerial teams. This experience is especially valuable for investment banks, which are an interesting source of information given their knowledge and expertise on investment management. Obviously, banking advice affects the capital structure of the company whose board they belong. From this point of view, bank directors encourage to borrow from the bank, both in the short term and in the long term. In addition, the amount of bank debt is higher when the bank does not maintain any other relationship with the company. This advisory role could even outrank the control of banking interests as a lender. Despite this, there is no unique relationship between banking directors and bank financing, owing to this relationship being affected by the characteristics of the financial system.

Second, a bank manager can become part of the board of a nonfinancial company to control or monitor their financial investment both in stock and in credit. In the first case, banks may act as any other shareholder trying to defend their interests as shareholders. Similarly, bank representatives may sit at the board to monitor firm's decisions and protect their interests as lenders, reducing the moral hazard in business–creditor relationship. Although the literature has found a positive relationship between the proportion of bank representatives and the firm leverage, this relationship can be understood in different ways. On the one hand, it could mean that credit institutions refuse lending when they are not compensated with a seat on the board. Alternatively, it could mean that financial intermediaries try to expand their monitoring abilities by controlling how firms manage the money they lend.

Third, the banking presence in the board of directors of industrial firms could be an attempt to expand the banking business. For example, banks could lend more money to firms in order to improve the knowledge or gain access to the sector in which the company operates. Likewise, financial institutions may expand the range of services they perform by selling complementary services as consulting and advising on mergers and acquisitions. All this set of relationships are summarized in Figure 3.24.

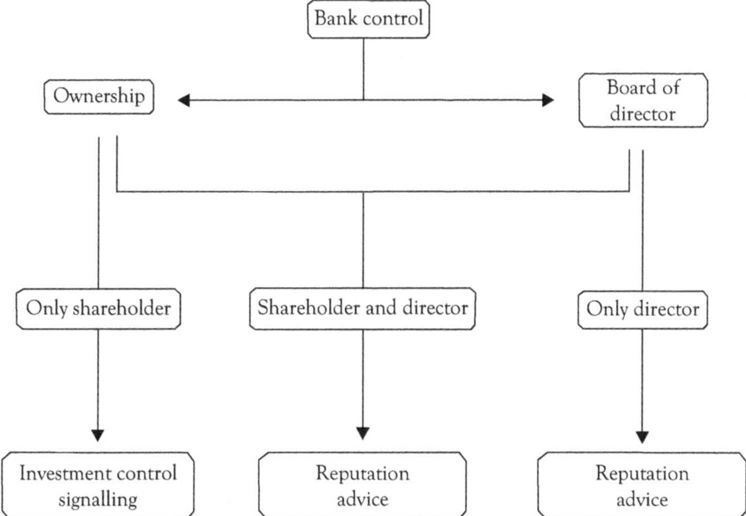

Figure 3.24 The role of banks in the governance of firms

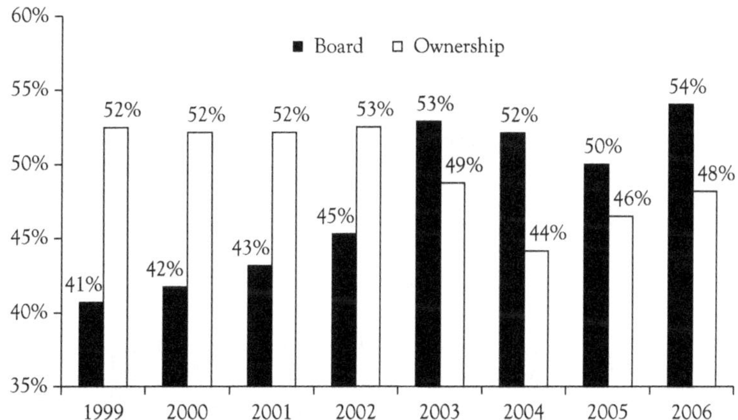

Figure 3.25 Evolution of the banking presence in the Spanish firms (I)

Source: Authors' calculation.

Note: Proportion of quoted firms with a bank either as shareholder or as director.

Figure 3.25 shows the percentage of nonfinancial firms with significant banking presence in the ownership or on the board of directors between 1999 and 2006. Banks play an important role in the governance of the Spanish large firms by being present in more than half of the companies.

Also, there is a certain evolution in the use of both mechanisms, because although the stock ownership has declined slightly over the years, it is increasingly common to have bankers on the board.

One can wonder whether this trend to the presence in the ownership of a smaller number of companies may be accompanied by the possession of higher levels of participation in each one. To answer this question, Figure 3.26 shows the proportion of total market capitalization held by banks and proportion of all the directors of listed firms who are banking representatives. Both proportions are divergent: Although in 1999 both values were, respectively, 16.2 percent and 12.4 percent, seven years later the values were of 10.1 percent and 12.3 percent. Consequently, we see a considerable reduction in the market capitalization of banking shares, together with a remarkable stability in the proportion of bank directors.

In the same vein, Table 3.14 compares the bank presence in 1999 and 2006, disaggregated by type of entity. The combined analysis of this table and Figure 3.25 shows that although the proportion of firms with banks as shareholders decreases from 52 percent to 48 percent, there was no parallel reduction in the number of banks in nonfinancial firms'

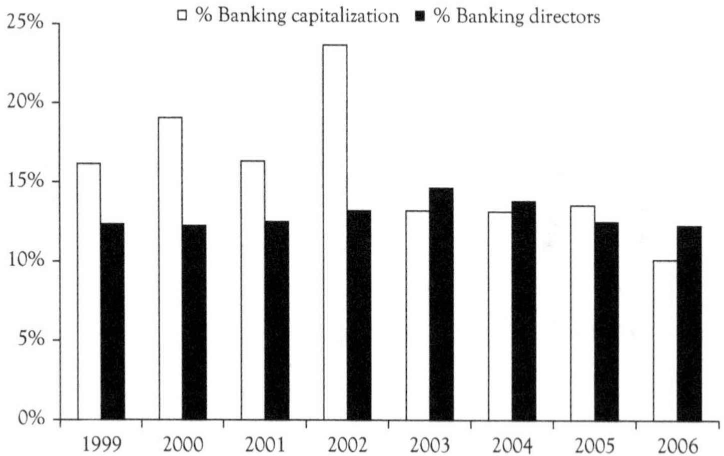

Figure 3.26 Evolution of the banking presence in the Spanish firms (II)

Source: Authors' calculation.

Note: Percentage of market capitalization accrued to the stake held by banks and percentage of all the directors of listed firms who are banking representatives.

ownership, but it increased from 39 to 42. That is, there are more entities in the capital of nonfinancial firms but with a trend to lower stakes. Therefore, there is not less involvement of banks in corporate governance, but a reorientation from an ownership-based presence to a board-based one (in fact, the number banks on boards increased from 33 to 46).

According to this table, we also see a significant presence of foreign banks in the ownership of Spanish firms, along with its more limited role in the boards. Because most foreign banks are investment banks, this figure confirms the lack of involvement of such entities in the governance of companies that they own. In addition, Spanish banks (excluding saving banks), mainly commercial or integrated in the universal banking, seem to prefer to participate in the board.

As previously explained, we can point out different arguments to explain the banking presence on the board when the bank is not a shareholder. A banking director can act as a financial expert to help the company raise funds, and their presence may also be due to the supervision of credit, in an attempt to reduce moral hazard. Also, the bank could take advantage of their presence on the board to provide other services to the company.

Table 3.14 also shows the role that savings banks have assumed. Unlike their traditional financial support to households and small businesses, they are nowadays the type of financial institutions whose presence in the governance of Spanish firms has grown to a greater extent, to the point of

Table 3.14 Evolution of the banking presence

		1999	**2006**
Ownership	Foreign banks	14	12
	Spanish banks	7	4
	Savings banks	18	26
		39	**42**
Board	Foreign banks	3	5
	Spanish banks	13	13
	Savings banks	17	28
		33	**46**

Source: Authors' calculation.

Note: Number and type of banks as shareholders or directors.

nearly two thirds of the banks institutions with ownership and more than half of which are present on the board of directors. Unlike other Spanish banks, savings banks tend to keep a balanced presence in both the ownership and on the board. This increased presence of savings banks is parallel to the growth in deposits and lending that they have experienced over the past two decades.

We must also mention that often the bank presence is not limited to a single entity. Thus, on average, the firms with bank shareholders have between 2.6 and 3.1 banks in the ownership (this value can be up to eight shareholders as in Iberia or Iberdrola). On the other side, firms with banking directors have on average between 2.7 and 3 entities represented (the maximum value is seven banks in the case of Actividades de Construcción y Servicios, S.A. ACS). From the perspective of banks, the entity with more frequent presence in the ownership of publicly traded companies is Banco Bilbao Vizcaya Argentaria, S.A. BBVA, present in 13 companies in 1999, whereas the bank that has more representatives sitting on other boards is Banco Santander Central Hispano, S.A. BSCH, with 14 directors in 1999.

In Table 3.15, we present an overview of the presence of banks in the governance of listed companies in 2006, indicating the number of firms in which the bank participates. Within each type, the first column corresponds to the ownership (O) and the second column to the board (B). The most active foreign bank, is Chase Bank, but it is limited to the ownership. Meanwhile, BBVA and BSCH are the banks with more presence on the boards, although the role of savings banks is more widely distributed.

Regarding the role of banks in Spanish economy, Andrés et al. (2010) show that the banks play a more or less active role in the governance of nonfinancial firms depending on the ownership and control structure of the firms. When the lending institution holds a position of control and its cash flow rights are not as strong as its control rights, it has a considerable capacity to profit from the situation to the detriment of the firm's value, particularly in settings that offer poor investor protection. In such contexts, banks display a predatory behavior that harms minority shareholders. In contrast, when another shareholder can take advantage of a position of power due to rights separation, the presence of banks proves

Table 3.15 ***Presence of banks in the ownership and the board of directors of Spanish listed firms***

Foreign banks	O	B	Commercial banks	O	B	Savings banks	O	B
Chase Bank	8		BBVA	6	12	La Caixa	7	7
Morgan Stanley	2		BSCH	2	10	CCMv	6	4
Credit Industriel et Commercial	1		B. Industrial de Bilbao	2		C. Guipúzcoa y San Sebastián	6	3
Goldman Sachs	1		B. Guipuzcoano	1	1	Caja Madrid	5	7
Lloyds Bank	1		B. Urquijo		4	Ibercaja	5	4
State Street Bank	1		Bankinter		2	C. Huelva y Sevilla	5	1
Banque Cantonale V.	1		Banca March		2	Caixanova	4	5
Bank of New York	1		Banco Pastor		2	Bancaja	4	4
Deutsche Bank	1		Banco Popular		2	Caja Granada	4	2
Caixa Capital Risco	1		Banco Gallego		1	Caja Galicia	3	6
Caixa General Depositos	1		B. Finantia Sofinloc		1	BBK	3	3
Barclays	1		B. de Comercio		1	Caja Murcia	3	2
Schroder Bank		1	B. Herrero		1	CAM	3	4
Merril Lynch		2	B. Zaragozano		1	Unicaja	3	3
HSBC		1				CajaAstur	3	2

(*Continued*)

Table 3.15 (Continued)

Foreign banks	O	B	Commercial banks	O	B	Savings banks	O	B
Itan Unibanco Holding		1				Cajasol	3	
Deutsche Postbank		1				Caja Badajoz	3	
						Caja Duero	2	3
						Caja Cataluña	2	2
						Caja Vital	2	2
						C. Municipal Burgos	2	2
						Caja Navarra	2	
						Caja España	1	3
						Caja Penedes	1	1
						Caja San Fernando	1	1
						CajaSur	1	1
						Caja Tarrasa		1
						CECA		1
						C. Santander y Cantabria		1
						EBN, Banco Negocios		2
						Participaciones Agrupadas		2

Note: Number of firms whose shares are partially owned by a bank (O) or in whose board there is a director representing banks (B).

beneficial to the firm's value. Therefore, in such cases, banks perform a supervisory function, acting as an efficient governance mechanism that is no doubt favored by their close ties to the firm.

3.3 Capital Structure in Spain

3.3.1 *Financial Leverage Structure*

Over three decades of research suggests that debt can act as a self-enforcing governance mechanism. Debt is a contract with costs and benefits. The benefit is usually the reduction in the agency cost, such as preventing the manager from investing in negative net present value projects, or forcing him to sell assets that are worth more in alternative use. The main costs of debt are that firms may be prevented from undertaking good projects because debt covenants keep them from raising additional funds, or they may be forced by creditors to liquidate when it is not efficient to do so.

In Figure 3.27, we compare nonfinancial Spanish firms leverage with the one of some countries with the same legal origin. In the previous years, Spanish firms' leverage is similar to that of German companies, but lower than the leverage of French, Portuguese, and Italian firms.

Next, we analyze what percentage of debt is supplied by banks (Figure 3.28). As we stated earlier, Spain is a bank-oriented economy,

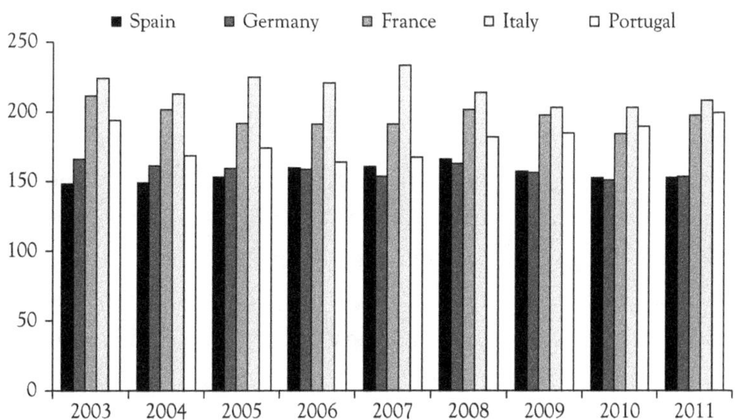

Figure 3.27 Nonfinancial firms' leverage

Source: Bank of Spain (2013).
Note: Total debt-to-equity ratio. Data in percentage.

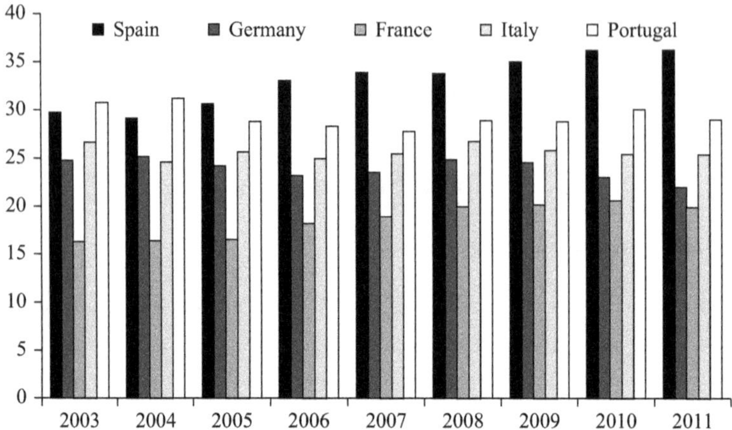

Figure 3.28 Nonfinancial firms' bank leverage

Source: Bank of Spain (2013).
Note: Bank debt-to-total debt ratio. Data in percentage.

which leads to a significant percentage of bank debt. This percentage exceeds 35 percent in the previous years, and it is higher than Portugal and Italy ratio and much higher than the one in Germany and France.

Because the interest rate of public debt is usually lower than that of bank debt—due to advantages of financial disintermediation—we should study the reasons explaining why firms borrow from banks. The set of possible explanations can be divided into four groups.

The first explanation is based on the asymmetric information or ex ante signaling problems. Asymmetric information in capital markets prevents lenders from knowing the real quality of the borrowers. In turn, good borrowers would make an effort to reveal the quality of their projects. From this perspective, banking debt acts as a signal from the companies with profitable growth opportunities, and this is why these firms prefer bank debt in spite of the higher interest rates of these funds. This same reason helps to understand why firms that are more widely known in capital markets or have a good reputation do not need to borrow from banks. Actually, firms relying on arm's length debt have been found to have worse reputation, to be younger or smaller than their counterparts in public debt markets (Krishnaswami et al. 1999; Nieto Sánchez and Tribó Giné 2000).

Closely related to the asymmetric information benchmark, we should note the easier access that creditors have to information from their borrowers. There may be some borrowers who are reluctant to reveal sensitive information about their projects because it could benefit their potential competitors. If this is the case, companies with profitable strategic projects would borrow from banks rather than from public capital markets because banks typically keep this information private and do not disseminate it.

The second group of reasons, although they are also based in information imperfections, refers to moral hazard or *ex post* information problems. Banks are usually able to monitor and control their borrowers in more detail than small, nonspecialized, and disperse lenders. Consequently, bank debt will have a positive impact when moral hazard and monitoring problems are more significant. One of the main *ex post* information drawbacks of debt is the problem of asset substitution, because borrowers have incentives to finance riskier projects. Discounting this possibility, lenders require borrowers to pledge some collateral in order to reduce default risk.

Furthermore, there are some other factors mentioned in the literature whose impact can also be explained from the moral hazard point of view. For instance, growth opportunities are supposed to enhance hidden actions because they allow a more opportunistic behavior of the managers. Consequently, firms with growth opportunities should primarily borrow from banks.

The third explanation has to do with transaction costs. Because debt issuance in capital markets usually has a high fixed cost, it is only worthwhile for large amounts of debt. This is another reason why large firms are more prone to public debt than small firms.

The last group of reasons concerns debt renegotiation. Public debt usually has harsher covenants than private debt, and banks are more likely than disperse creditors to roll over debt contracts in the case of default or bankruptcy. Given this difference between public and private debt, firms with a higher default risk would rather borrow from banks because debt renewals can avoid inefficient liquidations.

In spite of all these motivations, the choice between bank and public debt is not a static one; rather a dynamic perspective may be more suitable. More specifically, firms begin by borrowing from banks until they manage to build a good reputation as debtors. Once they have achieved it, they switch to public capital markets in order to take advantage of the lower debt cost due to their reputation.

Nevertheless, the analysis must take into account the legal and financial system of the country. In this sense, bank-oriented countries, such as Spain, have traditionally had a narrower relationship with banks than market-oriented ones, where the capital markets are usually more developed. Rajan and Zingales (1995) argue that the institutional characteristics that affect capital structure are tax code, bankruptcy laws, state of development of bond markets, and patterns of ownership. Similarly, López Iturriaga (2005) finds that the firms with less asymmetric information, more collateral, and more profitable are prone to borrow from public markets, whereas riskier firms are oriented to bank debt. At the same time, he shows that the financial management of firms is affected not only by the characteristics of the financial system, but also by legal features in each country. Actually, bank debt use differs among different countries conditional on the legal origin of their laws. His results stress that some aspects of the legal system, such as the protection of creditors, the requirements of information disclosure by firms, and the enforcement of the law, can have a significant influence on the ownership structure of corporate debt.

Miguel and Pindado (2001) developed a target adjustment model to explain firm characteristics that determine capital structure and how institutional features affect capital structure. They state that firms bear transaction costs when they decide to adjust their debt level. In the case of Spanish firms, the transaction costs are lower than those of U.S. firms, due to their higher percentage of private debt. Also they find an inverse relationship between nondebt tax shields and debt, which is more significant for Spanish firms than for U.S. ones, because they have more nondebt tax shields than U.S. firms. In addition, they show that the greater sensitivity of debt to fluctuations in cash flow when public debt ratio is high indicates that in countries such as Spain, where the bond market is inadequately developed, the advantage provided by private debt (in terms of lower agency costs of debt) is not as great as that provided by access to the bond market (fewer financing constraints). Also, it is important to take into account another institutional characteristic, such as the level of ownership concentration, because a high level mitigates the free cash flow problem, and therefore firms with highly concentrated ownership need to issue less debt.

3.3.2 *Cost of Debt*

Work on corporate governance and capital structure focuses on the association between governance and the cost of debt. When making investment decisions, debtholders estimate the firm's risk profile. The risk profile determines the required return by debtholders, which in turn is the firm's cost of debt. Debtholders try to estimate firms' default risk using all possible information available. One of its determinants is the quality of the firm's corporate governance. An increase in the quality corresponds to a decrease in the required risk premium by the debtholders. When studying the quality of corporate governance, lenders pay special attention to the shareholders' rights, range of takeover defenses, the degrees of transparency and responsibility toward the market, and finally to the Supervisory Board's structure and functioning. Firms scoring consistently high in these areas gain a good reputation as a result of which the required return by debtholders decreases (Blom and Schauten 2008).

A substantial body of empirical literature indeed confirms that the cost of debt can be affected by the quality of various governance mechanisms. Moreover, although most studies consider different governance components in isolation, it is quite possible that interaction effects occur. For example, Cremers et al. (2007) documented that shareholder control is associated with lower (higher) bond yields if the firm is protected from (exposed to) takeovers. Also Schauten and van Dijk (2011) find that firm's cost of debt is negatively related to the quality of disclosure but only if shareholder rights fall below a certain level.

Figure 3.29 shows the interest burden of nonfinancial firms in a set of bank-oriented economies. We observe that Spanish firms had the first years (2003–2006) the lowest interest burden among the countries considered. However, from 2007 the interest burden of Spanish nonfinancials increased strongly, just behind Portuguese's firms. Evidently, the financial crisis has to do a lot with that evolution.

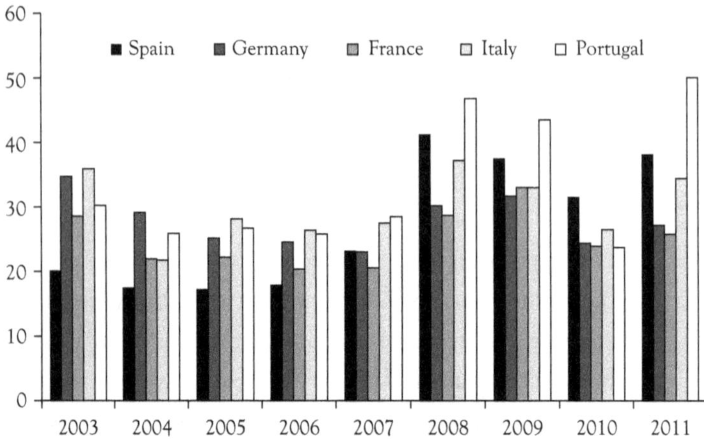

Figure 3.29 Firms' financial coverage

Source: Bank of Spain (2013).
Note: Interest expenses to earnings before interests and taxes. Data in percentage.

In this respect, we can also distinguish between bank debt and nonbank debt. The first have greater degrees of freedom, relative to nonintermediated, in that bank debt contracts can vary price (interest rate), maturity, collateral, and covenants terms and can also engage in lower cost renegotiation. In contrast, nonbank debt does not have the same monitoring access to private information (i.e., ability to reduce information asymmetry) and contracting degrees of freedom and hence price is more responsive to signals about the underlying risk and return characteristics of the firm, such as good corporate governance. However, although Spanish firms have the greater bank debt percentage (Figure 3.28), they also bear one of the highest costs of debt (Figure 3.29).

3.4 Dividends

The seminal research on dividend policy established that, in a frictionless world, when investment policy of a firm is held constant, its dividend payout policy has no consequences for shareholder wealth (Miller and Modigliani 1961). Higher dividend payouts lead to lower retained earnings and capital gains, and vice versa, leaving total wealth of the shareholders unchanged. However, contrary to this prediction, corporations follow extremely deliberate dividend payout strategies.

One of the most used approaches in the literature about this topic is the agency theory. In a world of significant agency problems between corporate insiders and outsiders, dividends can play a useful role. By paying dividends, insiders return corporate earnings to investors and hence are no longer capable of using these earnings to benefit themselves. Dividends could be better than retained earnings because the latter might never materialize as future dividends. In addition, the payment of dividends exposes companies to the possible need to come to the capital markets in the future to raise external funds, so this gives outside investors an opportunity to exercise some control over the insiders at that time.

There are no fully satisfactory theoretical agency models of dividends that derive dividend policies as part of some broad optimal contract between investors and insiders, which allows for a range of feasible financing instruments. Instead, different models capture different aspects of the problem. Moreover, the existing agency models do not fully deal with the issues of choice between debt and equity in addressing agency problems, the choice between dividends and share repurchases, and the relationship between dividends and new share issues.

In general, there are two alternative agency models of dividends. Both of them relate dividends with legal protection. The first perspective considers dividends as an outcome of legal protection of shareholders. Under this view, dividends are an outcome of an effective system of legal protection. Indeed, this perspective states that minority shareholders use their legal powers to force companies to return cash, thus avoiding insiders from using too high a fraction of company earnings to benefit themselves. Shareholders might do so by voting for directors who offer better dividend policies, or by selling shares to potential hostile raiders who then would gain control over non–dividend paying companies. Moreover, good investor protection makes asset diversion legally riskier and more expensive for insiders, thereby raising the relative attraction of dividends for them. So, the greater the rights of the minority shareholders, the more cash they extract from the company, other things equal.

In an alternative agency view, dividends are a substitute for legal protection. This perspective relies on the need for firms to come to the external capital markets for funds, at least occasionally. To do so on attractive terms, a firm must establish a reputation for moderation in expropriating shareholders. One way to establish such a reputation is by paying dividends, what reduces expropriation opportunities. A reputation for good treatment of shareholders is worth the most in countries with weak legal protection of minority shareholders, who have little else to rely on. As a consequence, the need for dividends to establish a reputation is the greatest in such countries. In countries with stronger shareholder protection, in contrast, the need for a reputational mechanism is weaker, and so is the need to pay dividends. This view implies that, other things equal, dividend policy ratios should be higher in countries with weak legal protection of shareholders than in those with strong protection.

La Porta *et al.* (2000a) found that the agency approach is highly relevant to an understanding of corporate dividend policies around the world. They find consistent support for the outcome agency model of dividends, thus, firms operating in countries with better protection of minority shareholders pay higher dividends. Moreover, in these countries, fast growth firms pay lower dividends than slow growth firms, consistent with the idea that legally protected shareholders are willing to wait for their dividends when investment opportunities are good. On the other hand, poorly protected shareholders seem to take whatever dividends they can get, regardless of investment opportunities.

In the next figures and tables, we analyze the evolution of the dividends in a country with a weak legal protection, such as Spain. Dividends play a very important role in Spanish Stock Market, although some companies have decided to interrupt the payment due to their poor financial situation. Nevertheless, the dividend return in Spanish Stock Market is one of the highest among developed countries, and significantly higher than the historic average in Spain (Figures 3.30 and 3.31). As Morgan Stanley reports, the average dividend yield among the main world stock markets is between 3 percent and 3.5 percent. Spanish companies try to compensate their shareholders because of the loss of wealth that comes from the important stock price falls in the previous years. Also, these higher dividends can be seen as an effort of Spanish firms to send a positive signal to the market, in a context of low investor protection.

Table 3.16 and Figure 3.32 show the different types of shareholders' remuneration in Spain. It should be noted that along 2013, 41.35 percent

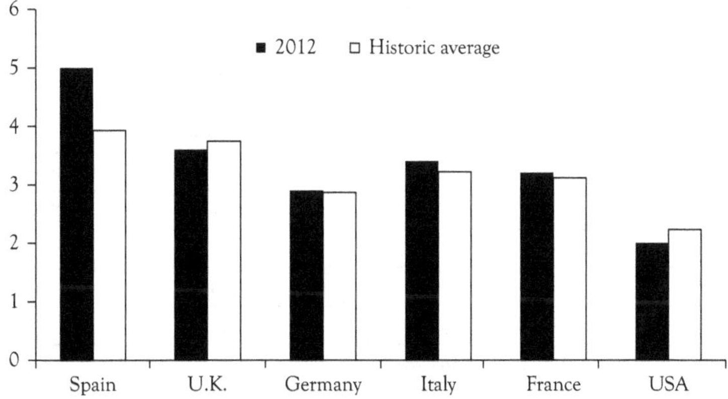

Figure 3.30 Dividend yields: international comparison

Source: Morgan Stanley Capital Investment (2013).
Note: Dividend-to-stock price ratio as a percentage.

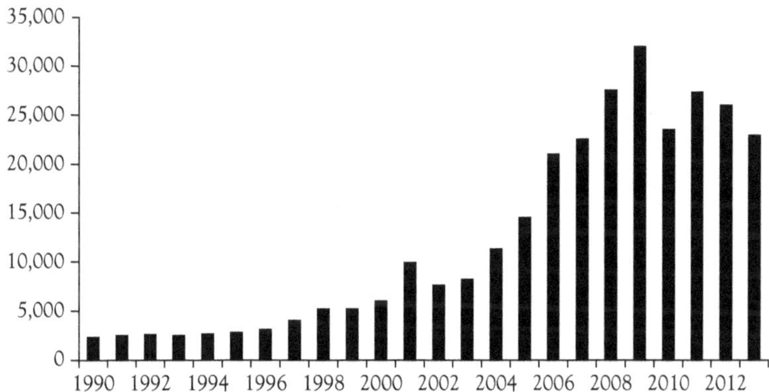

Figure 3.31 Total dividend payments

Source: Bolsas y Mercados Españoles (2014).
Note: Data in million euros.

of the remuneration was made by shares, most of them as script dividends, but also through other mechanisms such as the refund of issue premium. This percentage has been growing significantly, especially since 2009, due to the difficulties to get cash by the companies.

Table 3.17 shows the payout ratio of the listed companies in Spain. Although it has undergone continuous changes from 2004, due to the

Table 3.16 Payments to shareholders

Year	Dividends	Refund of issue premium	Capital decrease by refund of equity capital	Total
2000	7,011.70	51.23	323.43	7,386.36
2001	8,475.14	42.04	217.17	8,734.35
2002	8,446.78	28.78	223.79	8,699.35
2003	9,411.50	2,480.76	272.96	12,165.22
2004	11,678.02	2,288.84	208.54	14,175.40
2005	14,435.72	4,463.76	223.99	19,123.47
2006	21,809.71	513.02	761.24	23,083.97
2007	23,338.92	126.62	–	23,465.54
2008	28,065.00	346.56	–	28,411.56
2009	32,298.14	1,590.26	3.83	33,892.23
2010	24,288.33	295.26	9.32	24,592.91
2011	28,212.84	5,432.79	13.51	33,659.14
2012	26,768.81	384.46	13.51	27,153.27

Source: Bolsas y Mercados Españoles (2013).
Note: Data in million euros. In 2009, 2010, and 2011 dividends include the total amount paid in script dividends, both the exercised subscription rights, and those not exercised with a monetary value.

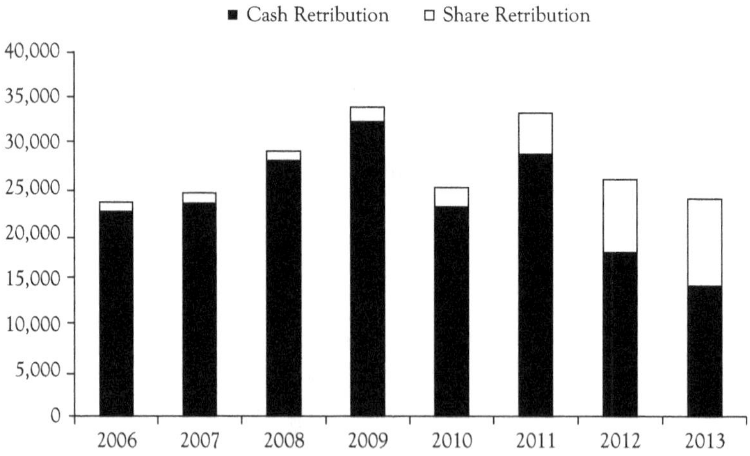

Figure 3.32 Shareholder compensation: cash versus repurchases

Source: Bolsas y Mercados Españoles (2014).
Note: Data in million euros.

erratic dividend policy of many (and important) firms, it displays values between 40 percent and 53 percent along the period considered. Actually, some important firms gave dividends over their net profit figures, hence with payouts over 100 percent. This is particularly common among banks, up to the point that the Bank of Spain has told lenders to limit the distribution of dividends in 2013 and subsequently because of the uncertain economic environment in Spain and the euro zone. More precisely, the Bank of Spain recommends that banks cap their cash dividends at 25 percent of net profit of the year. Although not obligatory, banks in Spain usually follow the banking regulator's recommendations.

By sectors, it shows off *Basic materials, industry, and construction*, which with a 57.12 percent payout, grew 41.42 percent between 2001 and 2012, and *Financial and real estate services* with a 57.26 percent payout and also a significant growth in the previous year. By contrast, *Oil and energy*, with a 30.43 percent payout, and *Technology and telecommunications*, 40.53 percent, are the sectors with lower figures. Especially it is very much remarkable to note the decrease in this last sector, from 103.38 percent in 2011 to 40.53 in 2012.

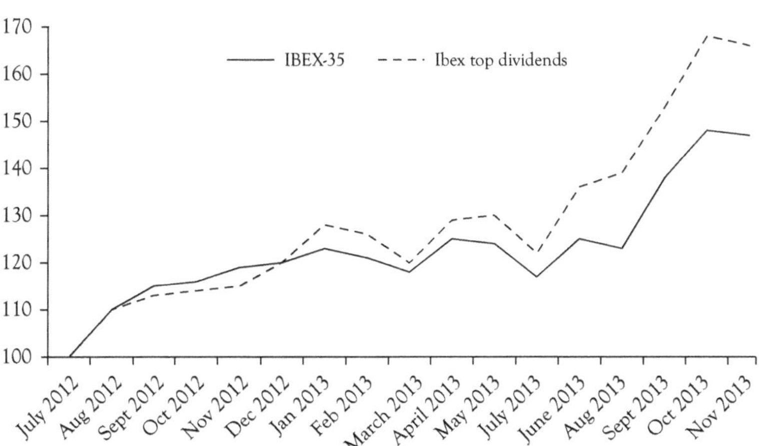

Figure 3.33 Comparison of IBEX-35 versus IBEX top dividend indexes

Source: Bolsas y Mercados Españoles (2014).

Note: Both the IBEX-35 and the IBEX top dividend indexes take 100 as the reference point in July 2012.

Table 3.17 Payout of the listed companies by sectors

Sector	2004	2005	2006	2007	2008	2009	2010	2011	2012
Oil and energy	43.40	48.53	47.98	49.59	68.17	45.07	26.89	36.40	30.43
Basic materials, industry, and construction	37.20	38.54	25.08	32.71	38.86	28.09	34.75	40.39	57.12
Consumer goods	42.69	45.69	50.32	46.78	50.58	50.32	44.68	54.31	48.76
Consumer services	54.74	64.69	49.24	54.29	51.65	54.88	86.15	69.67	47.78
Financial and real estate services	45.44	39.89	37.18	46.63	47.47	44.05	36.80	42.37	57.26
Technology and telecommunications	67.46	28.21	48.07	40.12	60.16	67.04	63.80	103.38	40.53
Total	**48.37**	**42.48**	**40.26**	**44.82**	**55.43**	**47.03**	**40.86**	**53.45**	**43.51**

Source: Bolsas y Mercados Españoles (2013).
Note: Data in percentage.

But does the market reward the firms with a greater dividend distribution? Figure 3.33 compares the evolution of the IBEX-35 index and the IBEX Top Dividend Index, which shows the growth of the 25 more profitable companies in terms of dividend yield in Spain. We can observe that in the previous year, market indeed rewarded those companies with a greater dividend, which had a greater growth in the value of the stock. It seems like the market considers the dividend distribution as a signal for a healthy financial situation of the firm.

CHAPTER 4

External Mechanisms of Corporate Governance in Spain

4.1 The Market for Corporate Control

The market for corporate control disciplines the managers of corporations with publicly traded stock to act in the best interests of shareholders. By buying up enough shares to vote in a new board of directors, a bidder can then replace a less-talented or unmotivated management team. The bidder profits when the new management team gets results, which can come in the form of improved corporate performance, higher profits, and, ultimately, higher share prices. The importance of the market for corporate control is very different across countries due to a number of historical and institutional factors. As Jensen (1993) states, the failure of the internal mechanisms of corporate control has resulted in a more and more important role of the external mechanisms, among which the market for corporate control plays an outstanding role (Cuervo 2002).

4.1.1 Legal Issues

The control of a Spanish listed company must be acquired by launching a takeover bid. Exceptionally, control gained through a merger may be exempt from the obligation to launch a takeover bid if it can be proved that merger was not carried out to control the target company. The control is supposed to have been acquired when at least 30 percent of the voting rights is reached. For the sake of the equal treatment, the terms of the offer must be the same for all holders of the securities to which the bid is addressed and who are in the same circumstances.

The main consents required to launch a takeover bid in Spain are the resolution of the bidder's managing body approving the takeover bid, the authorization of the takeover bid from the *Comisión Nacional del Mercado de Valores* (CNMV), the clearance from antitrust authorities (if required), and when the target company operates in a regulated sector, such as finance, energy, or telecommunications, the authorization from the relevant government agency.

Takeover bids may be mandatory or voluntary, although the boundaries between both types have been greatly blurred in recent laws. Conde (2013) explains that voluntary bids have several important advantages. First, in a voluntary bid the price can be freely determined by the bidder, whereas in a mandatory bid it must be approved by the CNMV. Second, in voluntary bids different types of compensation can be offered (i.e., cash, exchange of securities, or a combination of both), whereas mandatory bids must include a cash compensation. In addition, voluntary bids can be withdrawn more easily than mandatory bids.

From a legal perspective, it is possible to engage in a hostile acquisition in Spain. The difference between hostile and friendly bids (which, incidentally, is not a legal classification) depends on the position of the target company's board of directors in relation to the takeover bid. If the board of directors support the bid, it shall be considered to be friendly, whereas if the board does not back the bid, it shall be considered hostile.

In Spain, there are no specific rules governing the bidder's approach to the potential target company. Nevertheless, any agreement between the bidder and the target board must be disclosed in the bid prospectus and also mentioned in the report issued by the target company's board of directors. In any case, the attitude of the target board is vital for the success of a takeover bid. The board of directors and the management of the target company are prevented from taking any action that may frustrate or disrupt the success of a takeover bid, so as to ensure that the interests of shareholders prevail over their own interests. In spite of that, they can keep a critical ability to beat the bidder by searching for a competing offer or engaging in transactions aimed at causing the bid to fail, provided the general shareholders' meeting approves any such transactions.

In addition, once the takeover bid has been authorized by the CNMV, the target company's board must issue a report on the bid, which should state their position toward the bid. This statement can influence the decision taken by the target company shareholders.

The employees of the target company and the bidder are entitled to be informed of the bid as soon as it has been announced, and to receive the prospectus of the bid, once authorized by the CNMV. The prospectus must include extensive information on the bidder's corporate organization, ownership structure, activity, and financial situation, including net worth, turnover, total assets, financial liabilities and results, and information about the bidder's plans in relation to the target company's employment policy. The target company's employees shall also be provided with the report on the bid issued by the target company's board of directors. This report must include a discussion on the possible consequences of the bid and the plans of the bidder over the target company's employment.

According to Conde (2013), confidential negotiations between the bidder, the target company, or the target's main shareholders are allowed. However, special attention should be paid to the quotation of the target company shares and to the news relating to the company during the negotiation process. If any unusual development of the trading volume or the listing price of the target company is detected, or if there are any leaks about the negotiations, the bidder must immediately make public its intention to launch a takeover bid.

Although the bidder can purchase shares of the target company outside of the bidding process, these purchases in a listed company must be publicly disclosed when they result in the relevant shareholding reaching, or being reduced to 3 percent, 5 percent, and successive multiples of 5 percent up to 50, 60, 70, 75, 80, and 90 percent of the company share capital.

Broadly speaking, protectionism does not operate in favor of local owners. But in the sectors related to national defense, where investment from foreign buyers can be constrained on the basis of public interest, Spanish rules apply equally to both national and foreign buyers. This means that neither the Spanish Government nor the regulatory agencies have a protectionist attitude to foreign investments.

There is no standard duration for a takeover bid process, given that it depends on a number of factors. Nevertheless, a plain and simple takeover bid could take between 90 and 120 days to be completed from the time it is filed with the CNMV. The announcement of an intention to offer should be made as soon as the decision has been made by the bidder. In the case of mandatory offers, the announcement of the offer should be made without delay following the acquisition of control. Within one month of announcement, the bidder must submit a request for authorization to the CNMV. Once the CNMV receives the offer document and other complementary information, it must decide within seven business days whether the offer documentation satisfies the minimum requirements to be reviewed by the CNMV. If it does, the CNMV will authorize or reject the offer within 20 business days of filing. Within five business days of CNMV authorization, once the offer is authorized by the CNMV, the bidder must announce the terms of the offer, describing all of its essential features. In its announcement, the bidder must specify the applicable acceptance period, which must be no less than 15 calendar days and no more than 70 calendar days from the date of publication of the announcement.

Within 10 calendar days of the start of the acceptance period, the target company's management must issue a detailed and reasoned report responding to the offer. Within five business days from the end of the acceptance period, the Spanish stock exchange authorities communicate the total number of shares tendered into the offer in each exchange. Within two business days of receipt of the results, the CNMV aggregates and communicates the final results of the offer to the bidder, the target company, and the stock exchange authorities. On the third business day following announcement of the results, the offer consideration is settled in accordance with the rules of the Spanish clearance and settlement system. The CNMV will release the bank guarantee or cash deposit provided by the bidder in respect of any cash consideration only once the offer has been settled in full.

As far as the factors most likely to influence the outcome of the acquisition process are concerned, the consideration offered by the bidder is obviously the most critical one. Other important influences on the success of a bid are the need to obtain sector-related administrative approvals, the existence of competing bids and the defensive measures lawfully adopted by the target company.

4.1.2 Stylized Facts

Relative to its Anglo-Saxon counterparts, the Spanish market for corporate control is not so active and so big as in other countries. In Spain, as a bank-oriented country, the market for corporate control does not play such outstanding role as in other countries due to two main reasons: the size of the capital markets and the corporate ownership structure.

First, capital markets are not an outstanding source of funds for firms; they are less developed than in other countries. The low number of listed companies, along with the relative illiquidity of the market reduces the informativeness of stock prices and decreases significantly the possibility of success of hostile takeovers. As shown in Figure 4.1, the number of quoted domestic firms in Spain is not only lower than in the Anglo-Saxon countries such as the United Kingdom or the United States but also lower than its continental comparable counterparts such as Germany or Italy.

In terms of market capitalization, although the Spanish capital markets follow a similar pattern to the French or German one, the market capitalization is also lower than these markets. As shown in

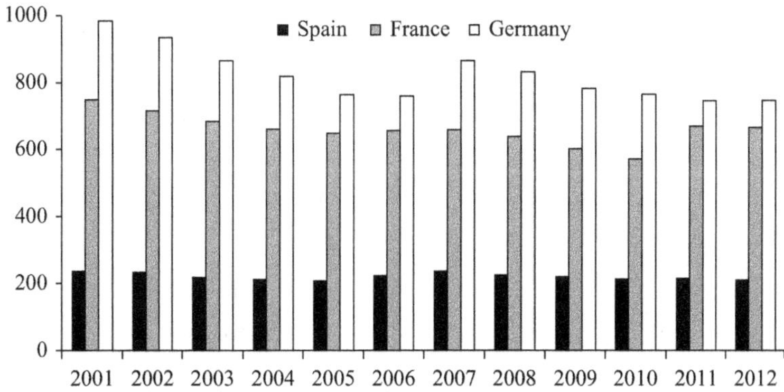

Figure 4.1 Number of listed firms

Sources: World Federation of Exchanges (www.world-exchanges.org/); World Bank (www.worldbank.org/); and Bolsas y Mercados Españoles (www.bolsasymercados.es/ing/home.htm).
Notes: Listed domestic companies are the domestically incorporated companies listed on the country's stock exchanges at the end of the year. The number of listed companies does not include investment companies, mutual funds, or other collective investment vehicles.

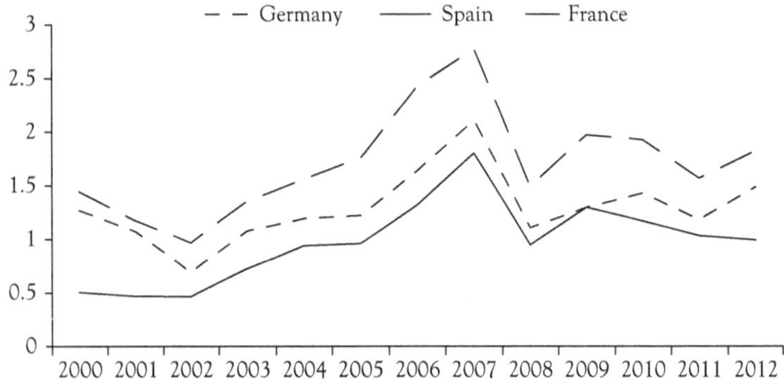

Figure 4.2 Market capitalization

Source: World Bank.
Note: Total capitalization of equity markets in Germany, Spain, and France. Data in billions of U.S. dollars.

Figure 4.2, in the first years of the 21st century the economic growth fueled the increase in the market capitalization of the euro area until reaching a peak in 2007. Nevertheless, the financial meltdown has meant a decrease of the market capitalization across Europe, resulting in Spanish capital markets having lower figures.

It should be highlighted that capitalization is concentrated in a relatively low number of companies. The two largest companies accounted for 29.4 percent of total capitalization of the Spanish market in 2012 and the 13 largest companies accounted for over 75 percent.

In Table 4.1, we compare the size of the Spanish market (measured in relation to the size of the national economy) with some of the major international markets. It can be seen that the ratio between capitalization and Gross Domestic Product (GDP) in Spain rose slightly in 2012. However, this ratio, which has suffered since the start of the crisis due to the sharp fall in prices in the Spanish market, remains low compared with the major international markets.

Despite the relatively low capitalization, the picture that emerges from the analysis of liquidity in Spanish markets is different. As shown in Table 4.2, the ratio based on trading stands at an average level compared with other internationally relevant markets although the significant fall suffered over the last year.

Table 4.1 Market capitalization as a percentage of nominal GDP

	2009	2010	2011	2012
USA[1]	104.4	118.2	103.7	119.0
New York	82	91.5	78.2	89.8
Japan[2]	67.3	71	57.2	66.9
London[3]	104.3	84.1	87.2	91.6
Euronext[4]	63.9	75	60.0	67.7
Germany	35.1	43.2	35.2	42.6
Spain	52.3	44.5	39.6	41.7

[1] The numerator is the combined total of the NYSE and NASDAQ.
[2] Includes data from the Tokyo and Osaka stock exchanges.
[3] The London data as from 2010 includes data from the Borsa Italiana, integrated in the London SE Group, and the GDP of both countries, after converting the Italian data to sterling pounds.
[4] The denominator is the sum of the nominal GDP of France, the Netherlands, Belgium, and Portugal.

Source: World Federation of Exchanges (www.world-exchanges.org/); International Monetary Fund (www.imf.org/); and CNMV (https://www.cnmv.es/).

In spite of this drop, the Spanish stock market was the fifth largest European market in terms of trading, after the Chi-X multilateral trading facility, the London Stock Exchange, NYSE Euronext, and the German Stock Exchange.

Analogous to the capitalization, the stock market trading is highly concentrated in a relatively low number of securities too. In 2012, the six most liquid securities in the market (BSCH, Telefónica, BBVA, Repsol, Inditex, and Iberdrola) accounted for over 75 percent of trading.

The second factor underlying the relatively lower development of the market for corporate control in Spain is related to the corporate ownership structure. As shown in the third section, Spanish quoted companies usually have a concentrated ownership structure with a group of blockholders or controlling shareholders.

This ownership structure goes hand in hand with some control-enhancing mechanisms as means to increase the control power of the main shareholders. In 2007, the Institutional Shareholders Services conducted a survey among 16 European countries on the proportionality between ownership and control in European Union listed companies. The study analyzes a list of control-enhancing mechanisms, which do

Table 4.2 Market trading as a percentage of nominal GDP

Country	2009	2010	2011	2012
USA[1]	212.3	208.2	204.0	148.1
New York	123.1	121.6	119.6	85.7
Japan[2]	81.2	70.2	69.6	60.8
London[3]	126.9	63.8	70.0	60.4
Euronext[4]	43.9	50.3	48.4	38.5
Germany	61	49.2	48.3	37.3
Spain	83.4	97	86.3	65.8

[1] The numerator is the combined total of the NYSE and NASDAQ.
[2] Includes data from the Tokyo and Osaka stock exchanges.
[3] The London data as from 2010 includes data from the Borsa Italiana, integrated in the London SE Group, and the GDP of both countries, after converting the Italian data to sterling pounds.
[4] The denominator is the sum of the nominal GDP of France, the Netherlands, Belgium and Portugal.

Sources: World Federation of Exchanges (www.world-exchanges.org/); International Monetary Fund (www.imf.org/); and CNMV (2011).

not follow the proportionality principle. Some of these mechanisms are used to allow existing blockholders to enhance control by leveraging voting power (diversions related to the one share, one vote principle and pyramid structures), other mechanisms can function as devices to lock-in control (priority shares, depository certificates, voting rights ceilings, ownership ceilings, and supermajority provisions), and other mechanisms are represented by coordination devices such as shareholders agreements.

According to this study, 62 percent of the Spanish surveyed firms had a control-enhancing mechanism. Furthermore, whereas 49 percent of the firms feature a single mechanism, 13 percent of the surveyed firms feature at least two mechanisms. The pyramidal structures and the coalitions of shareholders are the most often used mechanisms. As displayed in Figure 4.3, this survey shows that 45 percent of the companies have at least one significant shareholder who owns more than 20 percent of shares, and 17 percent of listed firms feature a pyramid structure.

Consistent with these data, Santana Martín (2010) reports that around 27 percent of quoted companies feature a coalition of shareholders. Coalitions of shareholders are defined by the Transparency Law (2003) as those agreements affecting the exercise of voting rights at general meetings, or that which constrain the free transfer of shares and bonds of

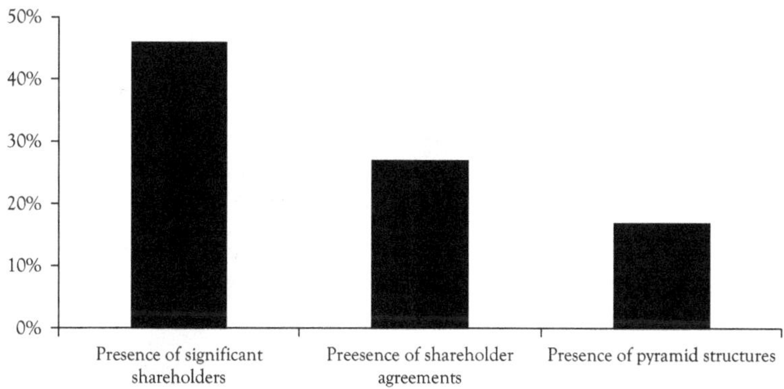

Figure 4.3 Control-enhancing mechanisms among Spanish firms

Sources: Institutional Shareholder Services (2007) and Santana Martín (2010).

listed companies. Likewise, The Royal Decree 1362/2007 defines acting in concert as an agreement whereby the parties use their voting rights to impose a common policy in connection with the company's management or to significantly influence its course.

Agreements can be grouped into four main categories: vote pooling and limitations on the free transfer of shares; vote pooling; limitations on the free transfer of shares; and composition of the board of directors or some other governing body, and setting of dividend policy. In Figure 4.4, we report the proportion of each category on the whole list of coalitions.

These agreements account for more than 45 percent of voting shares. As shown in Table 4.3, although the proportion of voting rights implied in the coalition is quite steady, there is an increasing trend in the proportion of firms with such kind of mechanisms: In 2003 only 15 percent of the firms featured a shareholder coalition, whereas in 2011 this proportion has almost doubled up to 28 percent.

The use of shareholder coalitions is significantly different from the voting agreements in the U.S. market or the analysis of the divergence between control rights and cash flow rights in a number of ways. First, these agreements are more transparent given the publicity requirements imposed by the CNMV. Second, the dominant owners who have effective control of the company take the lead in the shareholder agreements. These agreements do not require the transfer of shares to an involved shareholder but rather implies an explicit commitment that coalition

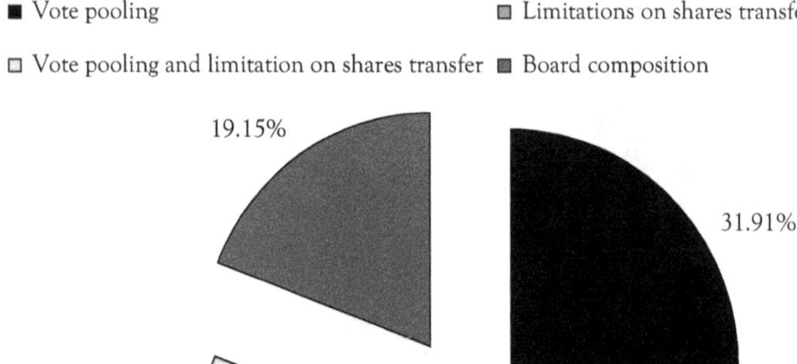

Figure 4.4 Types of shareholder coalitions

Source: CNMV (2011).

Table 4.3 Shareholder coalitions in Spanish firms

	2003	2005	2007	2009	2011
% Firms with coalitions	15.85	20.00	30.36	23.67	28.42
% Voting rights in the coalition	44.96	41.09	46.89	42.65	45.85

Source: Santana Martín (2010).

members will vote with the dominant owner or will limit the transfer of shares outside the coalition. Third, coalitions improve the stability of the ownership structure because they are often signed for a period not shorter than two years and can be rolled over. Four, the coalitions do not generate an internal market among the divisions of the same firm as the pyramid structures do. In addition, the Spanish law, by requiring the identification of the members, allows knowing the composition of the controlling group in actual terms and not in terms of likelihood (i.e., the group of shareholders most likely to form a coalition) as some of previous research does.

Although there is a widespread use of shareholder coalitions in many countries, Spain provides a unique opportunity for this analysis because since 2003 listed firms must report certain information on shareholder coalitions. The Improvement of the Transparency in Quoted Firms Law 26/2003 explicitly allows the agreements among shareholders that modify the voting rights in the general shareholders meeting or that constraint the transmissibility of shares. In so doing, the shareholders voluntarily accept to limit their votes or their ability to sell the shares. These agreements must be published in the corporate website and also must be notified to the CNMV. This announcement must show who the shareholders involved in the agreement are, the proportion of shares involved, and the content of the agreement (i.e., limitation of votes or limitation of shares sales).

Shareholder coalitions can play a dual role. On the one hand, control-enhancing shareholder coalitions have a beneficial effect on minority shareholders' wealth by improving significant shareholders' ability and incentives for managerial control and on the other, they enable a balanced power among the dominant owner and other large shareholders. This control-enhancing role is more important in countries with less liquid capital markets and where legal and political factors constrain the market for corporate control. In addition, coalitions can also be an efficient control mechanism in countries such as Spain with weak legal protection of minority shareholder by enhancing the contest to the power of other large shareholders against the dominant owner's control.

On the contrary, self-dealing shareholder coalitions empower the dominant owners to such an extent that they can become entrenched and can extract private benefits at the expense of nonparticipating shareholders. In this scenario, coalitions may exacerbate the conflicts of interest among shareholders by conferring too much power to a few entrenched owners. Furthermore, in some legal environments of high ownership concentration, dominant owners are usually linked to managers by family, business, or other kinds of group ties. Hence, the entrenchment of shareholders can mean, to some extent, the entrenchment of managers.

The thorough analysis of Santana Martín (2010) provides certain insights into some characteristics of the shareholder coalitions among Spanish firms. More specifically, this author shows significant differences

Table 4.4 Shareholder coalitions and firm characteristics

		% Firms	% Voting rights			% Firms	% Voting rights
Size	Large	35.85	44.72	Takeover provisions	More	26.67	29.95
	Small	18.17	29.62		Fewer	32.89	43.16
Ownership	Concentrated	32.68	51.18	Ownership pyramids	Yes	28.33	40.34
	Dispersed	21.82	22.99		No	25.53	38.35

Source: Santana (2010).

among firms in terms of size, ownership concentration, anti-takeover provisions, and the pyramid structure.

As shown in Table 4.4, large firms feature shareholder coalitions almost twice as often as small quoted firms (35 percent vs. 18 percent) and the proportion of involved voting rights is significantly higher. The firms with concentrated ownership also have more coalitions than their dispersed ownership counterparts and, more importantly, the difference in the proportion of voting rights is even higher than in the previous case. Given the possible conflicts of interests between dominant shareholders and minority shareholders, the data from Table 4.4 can mean that large shareholders in the firms with concentrated ownership use the coalitions as an enhancing mechanism in order to increase their power and become entrenched.

The comparison of the firms with anti-takeover provisions provides interesting insights too. We can see that firms with defensive measure against takeovers feature less coalitions than their counterparts. It could mean that shareholder coalitions are an alternative protection measure, so that they become more necessary when the firms have fewer provisions.

In the same vein, firms have different attitude toward shareholder coalitions depending on the pyramid structures. We must keep in mind that these structures are control-enhancing mechanisms that allow the separation between voting rights and cash flow rights through a number of intermediate firms. As shown in Table 4.4, shareholder coalitions are

Table 4.5 Anti-takeover measures in Spanish corporate by-laws

Voting right ceilings	Restriction to the voting rights held by a single shareholder (usually 10%).
Supermajority votes	A level of approval for specified actions higher than the minimum set by the Spanish general law. Such provisions often establish approval levels of 75% or 90% for actions that otherwise would require simple majority approval (mergers and acquisitions, stock issuance, and others).
Seniority of directors	Need to have been shareholder for a certain time to be elected as director.
CEO seniority	Need to have been director for a certain time to be elected as chairman of the board.
Staggered boards of directors	Boards in which directors are divided into separate classes and elected to overlapping terms.

Source: Santana and Aguiar (2007).

more frequent in firms with pyramid structures. As far as the family nature of the firm is concerned, family firms do not use the shareholder coalitions differently from the nonfamily firms.

As far as anti-takeover provisions are concerned, Santana and Aguiar (2007) and Ruiz and Santana (2009) provides an exhaustive survey of this instrument in the Spanish quoted firms. They thoroughly analyze the corporate by-laws of all the listed firms and define the five provisions summarized in Table 4.5.

These provisions can be considered as internal control provisions because they increase a large shareholder's cost of exercising control or influencing corporate policies, which therefore directly affect the internal market for control. By imposing costs on large shareholders, however, these mechanisms also can impede external bids for control.

Based on these provisions, Santana and Aguiar (2007) compute an index of takeover protection. This index is defined as the sum of five dummy variables, each one equaling one whether the corporate by-laws allow each one of the provisions. Thus, the index of takeover protection oscillates between zero and five. The higher the index, the more entrenched the managers against possible takeovers.

As shown in Figure 4.5, the proportion of Spanish firms with anti-takeover provisions in their corporate by-laws has declined slightly in recent years. In 1996, 42.3 percent of firms had anti-takeover provisions,

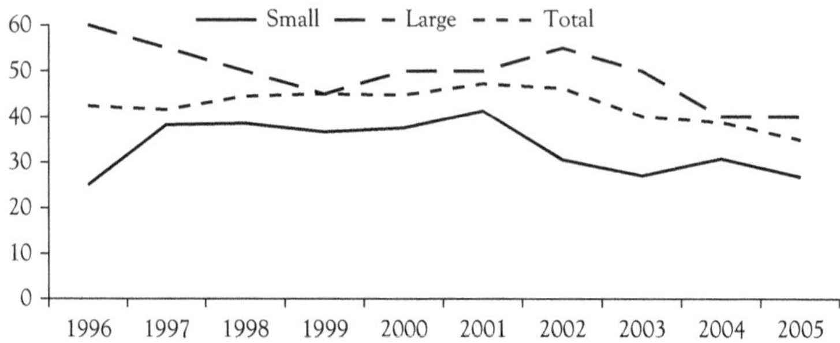

Figure 4.5 Percentage of firms with anti-takeover provisions

Source: Santana and Aguiar (2007).

whereas in 2005 (the latest year with available information), it amounted to 34.9 percent. More importantly, there has been a clear reduction in the number of firms with provisions since 2003, which can be attributed to the enactment of the Improvement of the Transparency in Quoted Firms Law 26/2003. There are also some differences due to the size of the firm because larger firms usually have more provisions than their smaller counterparts.

Figure 4.6 shows that the proportion of firms with defensive measures depends also on the ownership concentration. Whereas firms with high-concentrated ownership used to have more provisions, the recent trend in capital markets has resulted in a convergence process, so that there are no significant differences between both kinds of firms after 2003.

The takeover protection index follows a similar pattern (Figure 4.7). The number of defensive measures has not only decreased during the 1995–2005 period but also experienced a sharp decline after 2003 due to the improvement in the information requirements in the Spanish capital markets. Regarding the effect of the firm size, there is a clear convergence between large and small firms.

In Figure 4.8, we show the distribution of the protection index. We report the proportion of firms with anti-takeover measures depending on the number of provisions in their by-laws. One must take into account that these proportions are calculated only on the firms that actually have protective measures. The percentage of firms with a single measure increased from 50 percent in 1995 to 69.4 percent in 2005. On the

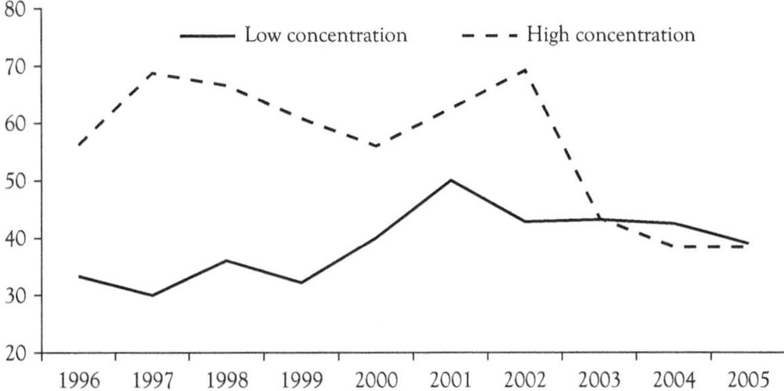

Figure 4.6 Ownership concentration and anti-takeover provisions

Source: Santana and Aguiar (2007).

Percentage of firms with anti-takeover provisions depending on the ownership structure. Low (high) concentration firms are those in which the voting rights of the largest shareholder are below 20 (over 50) percent.

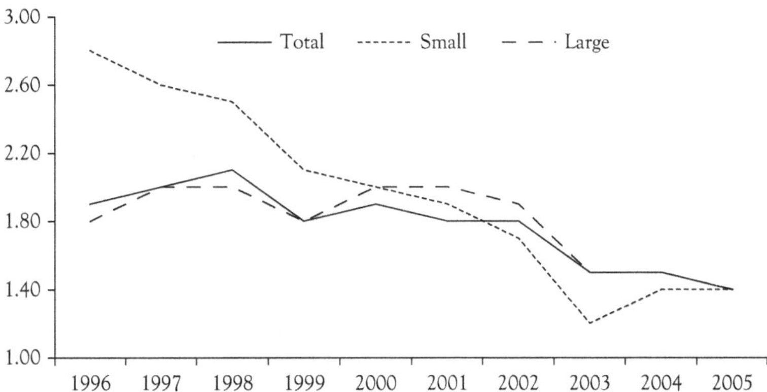

Figure 4.7 Evolution of the index of takeover protection

Source: Santana and Aguiar (2007).
Notes: Average number of anti-takeover provisions depending on the ownership structure. Low (high) concentration firms are those in which the voting rights of the largest shareholder are below 20 (over 50) percent.

contrary, the proportion of firms with three or more provisions decreased from 27.2 percent to 11 percent in the same period. The proportion of firms with two protective provisions in their by-laws remained steady around 20 percent.

As far as the types of provisions actually implemented are concerned, Figure 4.9 shows that the voting rights ceilings are the most usual measure with 44 percent of the companies using this provision. The second most usual provision is supermajority votes, although there has been a decline

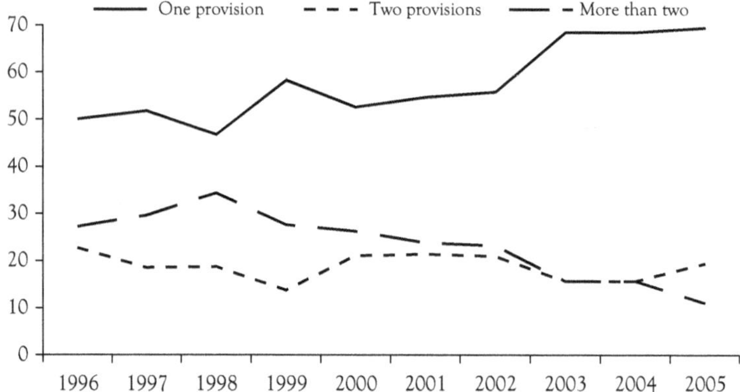

Figure 4.8 Distribution of the index of takeover protection

Source: Santana and Aguiar (2007).
Note: Number of anti-takeover measures in the corporate by-laws (in percentage).

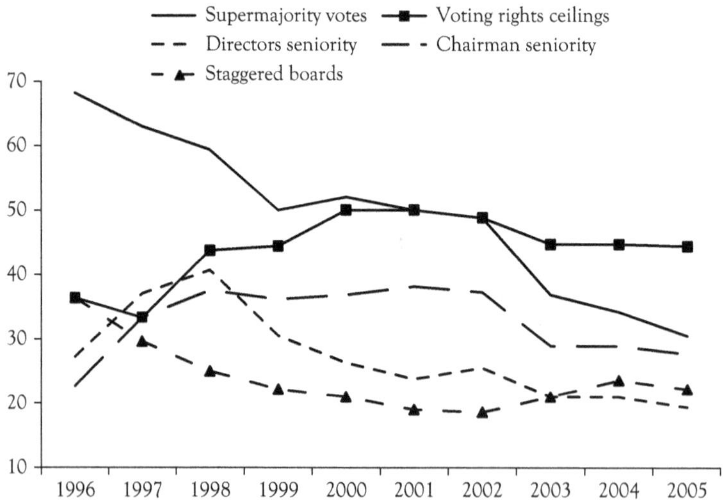

Figure 4.9 Anti-takeover provisions actually implemented

Source: Santana and Aguiar (2007).
Note: Percentage of firms with each anti-takeover provision.

in the proportion of firms with this measure in their corporate by-laws: In 1996, 68.1 percent of the companies that had protective measures used this provision, whereas in 2005, the proportion had fallen to 30.5 percent. Once again, we can see that 2003 is an inflexion point and the proportion of provisions decreases after 2003.

Given these characteristics of the Spanish capital markets (both the low size of the market and the specific measures adopted by the firms) it comes with little surprise the low activity of the market for corporate control. In Figure 4.10, we report the number and the value of takeovers among listed firms. This figure suggests two conclusions. First, the low number of takeovers related to the whole population of listed firms. Second, in spite of this low number, there is a steady declining trend in the number of operations. As far as the amount is concerned, with the exception of the 2006 to 2007,[1] there has not been such a declining trend as in the number of takeovers.

Figure 4.11 provides additional information about the number and the value of announced mergers and acquisitions with Spanish participation (both among quoted and nonquoted firms). Contrary to the situation of their listed counterparts, the market for mergers and acquisition among

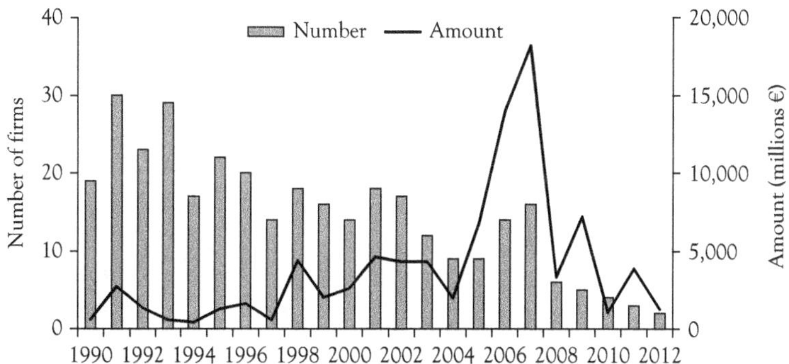

Figure 4.10 Takeovers among listed firms

Source: CNMV (2011).

[1] In these years, two significant Spanish firms (Altadis and Endesa) were taken over by foreign companies (Enel Energy and Imperial Tobacco).

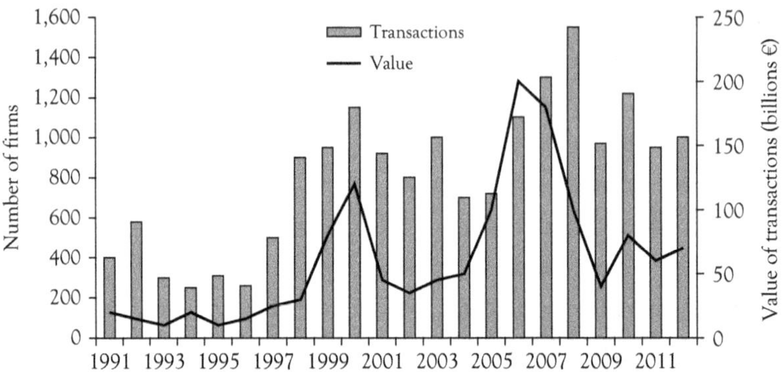

Figure 4.11 Number and value of announced mergers and acquisitions

Source: Institute of Mergers (www.imaa-institute.org) and Acquisitions and Alliances.

nonlisted firms has been more active in the latest 10 years than it used to be during the 1990s decade. In any case, the mergers and acquisitions involving Sp firms is significantly lower than in most of the countries of Western Europe.

4.2 External Audit

The market for audit services in Spain started with the implementation of the 8th Directive on Company Law (García and Argilés, 2013). With the main goal of increasing the reliability of the company's financial statements, the Spanish Audit Law was enforced in 1988. This law established the obligation for companies above a certain size to appoint an external auditor to issue a report about the company's financial statements.

To safeguard auditor independence, the Spanish Audit Law established a set of criteria to regulate the auditor–client relationship. Accordingly, a multiyear contract was established with a length ranging between three and nine years. In addition, irrespective of the length of the initial contract, the reelection of the audit firm was not allowed. The imposition of a limit in the number of years a company could be audited by the same firm was equivalent to establish a mandatory auditor rotation rule. Nevertheless, both the limit on the maximum number of years to be audited by the same firm, and the prohibition to renew the audit contract were abolished after a legal reform in 1995.

After more than 20 years, the Spanish Audit Law has been updated and modified with a new Audit Law (12/2010). This new legal framework has aimed to strengthen the reliability of auditing and promote a homogenous environment in Europe. The new law adapts the Spanish Audit Law to the changes that have taken place in Spanish corporate–commercial and accounting law in recent years. It also amends the liability system for auditors, who must assume full liability in relation to consolidated financial statements or accounting documents, meaning that their liability cannot be restricted to the group companies that had been audited by them.

The new law specifies the system of legal sources that must be used in performing the audit, which will be audit standards, ethical rules, and the rules governing the internal quality assurance system of auditors and audit firms. With respect to audit standards, it introduces the international audit standards that will be adopted by the European Commission, and keeps the Spanish audit standards in force until those international standards are adopted.

A characteristic of the new law is that it reduces the public disclosure period for audit standards before they are published by the Accounting and Audit Institute from six to two months. Audits can be performed by persons authorized in another EU member state and by auditors from other countries who are registered. The registration in the Official Auditors' Register is compulsory for auditors and audit firms who issue auditor's reports in relation to the financial statements of certain companies domiciled outside the EU, whose shares are admitted for trading in Spain.

Auditors must observe the duties of independence and secrecy in performing audits. The audit regulations clarify the set of actions that must be performed by auditors in the observance of their duty of independence, and delimit the causes that lead to incompatibility for them. The duty of secrecy extends to anyone taking part in the performance of audits. Auditors must be and appear to be independent from the companies they audit in the performance of their functions. Thus, they must refrain from acting when their objectivity in relation to the review of accounting documents could be jeopardized. Independence will be understood as the absence of interests or influences that may undermine the auditor's objectivity. To assess a possible lack of independence, the performance of other services to the audited company that may limit the auditor's objectivity must be taken into account. However, with the exception of services consisting of accounting activities, the rest of the services, such as consulting or tax advice, would not imply, in principle, the auditor's incompatibility.

As a consequence of a clearer and clearer legal framework, the audit services have expanded in Spain in recent years (Figure 4.12).

As in many other countries, the audit market of publicly traded companies is highly concentrated in a situation characterized by the oligopoly of the so-called Big Four audit firms (KPMG, PricewaterhouseCoopers, Deloitte, and Ernst & Young). Although this situation seems to be widely spread across Europe, Spain is one of the countries with a more concentrated audit market (Table 4.6).

In fact, in November 2011, the European Commission issued the proposal for a regulation on the quality of audits of public-interest entities and for a directive to enhance the single market for statutory audits. These new rules are a consequence of the financial crisis that has highlighted weaknesses in the statutory audit, especially with regard to banks and financial institutions. Concerns around conflicts of interest have been expressed as

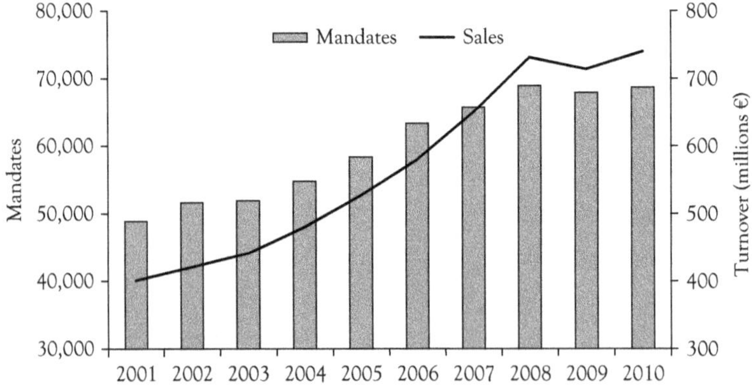

Figure 4.12 Audit services

Source: Crespo (2012).

well as the potential for an accumulation of systemic risk as the market is effectively dominated by the Big Four companies.

The proposals regarding the statutory audit of public-interest entities, such as banks, insurance companies, and listed companies, envisage measures to enhance auditor independence and to make the statutory audit market more dynamic. One of the key measures in this respect is a mandatory rotation of audit firms, so that audit firms will be required to rotate after a maximum engagement period of six years. Joint audits are not made obligatory but are encouraged. Audit firms will be prohibited from providing nonaudit services to their audit clients. In addition, large audit firms will be obliged to separate audit activities from nonaudit

Table 4.6 Concentration of the audit market

Member state	Number of companies	CR1 (%)	CR4 (%)	CR8 (%)	HHI
Austria	75	36	83	99	2,281
Belgium	151	32	88	100	2,256
Bulgaria	218	18	50	76	873
Cyprus	112	32	94	98	2,737
Denmark	167	53	96	100	3,493
France	761	24	81	97	1,831
Germany	781	40	97	98	3,244
Ireland	40	40	98	100	2,995
Italy	269	40	98	100	2,786
Netherlands	135	34	91	100	2,353
Spain	155	58	99	100	4,050
Sweden	391	48	99	100	3,437
United Kingdom	2061	43	98	100	2,884
EU average	**391**	**38**	**90**	**98**	**2,709**

Source: Le Vourc'h and Morand (2011).

Notes: Market share by the largest, two largest and four largest audit firms, and the Hirschman-Herfindahl index (HHI) of concentration. The HHI is one of the most often used indexes to measure concentration. It is based on the total number and size distribution of firms. It ranges from 1/N to 1, with N the total number of firms in the market. For a more convenient reading HHI can be computed on a base of 10,000. The United States Antitrust Division Merger Guidelines provide the following classification: not concentrated markets (HHI below 1,500), moderately concentrated markets (HHI between 1,500 and 2,500), and highly concentrated markets (HHI above 2,500).

activities in order to avoid all risks of conflict of interest. Enabling auditors to exercise their profession across Europe, the Commission proposes the creation of a Single Market for statutory audits by introducing a European passport for the audit profession. To this end, the Commission proposals will allow audit firms to provide services across the EU and to require all statutory auditors and audit firms to comply with international auditing standards when carrying out statutory audits.

As previously stated, Spain is not an exception in the landscape of audit concentration (Monterrey and Sánchez, 2008; Ruiz Barbadillo et al., 2009). Table 4.7 reports the market share of the Big Four both for nonlisted and listed audit firms. There is a big imbalance between the audit market of nonlisted and listed firms. As it can be seen, the market for nonlisted firms (namely, small and medium enterprises) is much more diversified than the audit market of the quoted firms (basically, large firms).

To provide a more simple idea of the concentration of the audit market, Figure 4.13 reports the market share of the Big Four in 2010, and Table 4.8 reports the turnover of the 10 largest audit firms in 2009. Once again, we can see the gap between the four largest firms and the following ones.

To corroborate the concentration of the audit market in Spain, Table 4.9 provides a comparison of the concentration index of *n* degree between 2001 and 2010. This concentration index measures the market share accrued to the *n* largest audit firms. Consistent with previous

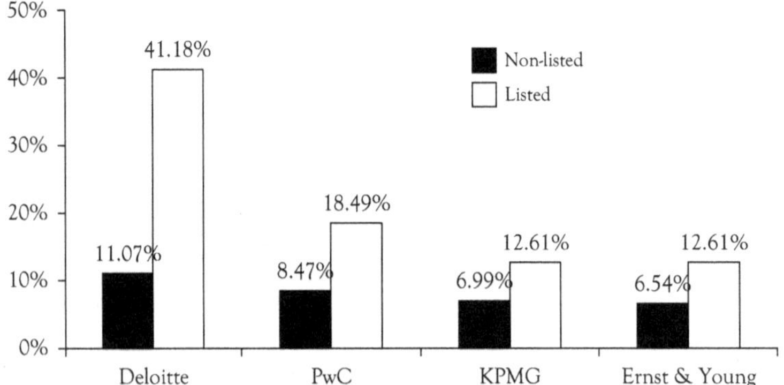

Figure 4.13 Big Four market share

Source: Crespo (2012).

Table 4.7 Market share (in %) of the Big Four audit firms

	2000	2001	2002	2003	2004	2005	2006	2007	2008	2009	2010
	Non-listed										
Deloitte	13.78	13.33	12.15	10.96	10.96	10.68	10.71	10.79	10.73	10.89	11.07
PwC	10.14	9.91	10.02	9.50	9.03	8.39	7.92	8.09	8.53	8.09	8.47
KPMG	5.71	5.84	6.38	6.87	6.81	6.77	7.17	6.88	6.89	7.18	6.99
Ernst & Young	5.89	5.89	6.34	6.81	6.72	7.01	6.81	6.84	6.68	6.32	6.54
Big Four	35.52	34.98	34.89	34.13	33.52	32.84	32.62	32.59	32.82	32.49	33.06
	Listed										
Deloitte	38.10	40.74	41.05	41.41	35.29	38.68	40.91	39.82	37.61	38.14	41.18
PwC	25.40	22.22	21.05	19.19	19.61	16.98	16.36	18.58	19.66	18.64	18.49
KPMG	12.70	12.35	10.53	11.11	11.76	12.26	12.73	11.50	11.97	12.71	12.61
Ernst & Young	9.52	9.88	12.63	12.12	14.71	14.15	14.55	14.16	15.38	14.41	12.61
Big Four	85.71	85.19	85.26	83.84	81.37	82.08	84.55	84.07	84.62	83.90	84.87

Source: Crespo (2012).

Table 4.8 Distribution of the audit market

Firm	Turnover	Firm	Turnover
Deloitte	437	Grant Thornton	58
PwC	410	Praxity	33
KPMG	307	Mazars	33
Ernst & Young	278	Horwath	28
BDO	86	Moore Stephens	24

Source: Le Vourc'h and Morand (2011).
Note: 2009 revenues of the top 10 audit firms (millions €)

Table 4.9 Concentration index (in %) in the audit market

	2001	2010
C1	38.10	41.18
C2	63.50	59.67
C3	76.20	72.28
C4	85.72	84.89
C5	87.52	86.59
C6	89.22	88.29
C7	90.52	89.29
C8	91.02	90.29
C9	91.32	90.89
C10	91.72	91.39
C20	93.3	93.4
C50	96.4	96.5
C100	98.1	97.9

Source: Crespo (2012) and Le Vourc'h and Morand (2011).

information, there is a clear gap between the Big Four and the other firms. In addition, in dynamic terms, the concentration on the Big Four has not changed significantly in these 10 years, and they still account for approximately 85 percent of the market of large firms.

Conclusion

How corporations are governed is one of the topics that have attracted most the attention of the academia, the policy makers, and the practitioners in the recent years. In this book, we show a primer of the corporate governance in Spain. Spain is considered a civil-law country with a bank-oriented financial system in which banks play an active role relative to markets. But, while the size of financial intermediaries is near the international standards, nonbank intermediaries are much less important in Spain than in other Europeans countries, which renders a bank-centered model of financial organization.

Currently, the Spanish financial system is going through a process of deep restructuring and consolidation due to the financial crisis. This process has modified the landscape of the banking system, which was characterized by the heterogeneous kinds in the legal status of banks. The former savings banks, namely, private foundations with a board of trustees with representatives from regional authorities, city halls, workers, depositors, and nonprofitable founding entities, have been the core of a wave of mergers and acquisitions that has dramatically decreased the number of financial intermediaries. This change has not affected the outstanding role played by banks and their close ties with the governance of nonfinancial firms. Banks in Spain are not only creditors, but also reference shareholders or sit at the board of directors of nonfinancial firms.

Most of the corporate governance issues in Spain have emerged in the 1990s and have come hand in hand with European Union initiatives and recommendations. Indeed, the codes of good governance are strongly influenced by the ones developed in other European countries. Thus, the effectiveness of the Spanish corporate governance system is affected by the differences between the environment where they were set up (normally Anglo Saxon origin countries with a market orientation) and the Spanish national framework where they apply.

Because of the bank orientation, the corporate governance system relies heavily on the so-called internal mechanisms of governance (i.e., large shareholders and the board of directors). As in other Continental European countries, the controlling shareholders mitigate the conflict between management and minority shareholders, but instead another conflict arises between controlling shareholders and minority shareholders.

Regarding ownership structure, Spanish firms show a concentrated ownership with a significant presence of families and banks. Large controlling shareholders frequently own substantially more control rights than cash flow rights, which gives them a high expropriation potential. This fact explains the attention that policy makers have paid recently to the protection of minority shareholders.

As the previous codes of good governance, the latest Unified Code of Governance focuses on the role of the board of directors. Following the international trends, this last issued code emphasizes some characteristics as the size and composition of the board, its different committees, and the compensation structure of the directors. However, it omits other issues that could also have a significant impact on the board effectiveness such as the qualification and engagement of individual directors, the boardroom dynamics, and the processes by which the board fulfills its duties.

The firms' financial characteristics have also a relevant influence as internal mechanisms of control. As far as the capital structure is concerned, the level of financial leverage among Spanish firms is not different from the other Continental European countries. Nevertheless, coherently with the importance of banks, the proportion of banking debt in Spain is higher than in the European counterparts. In the same vein, dividends work as a mechanism of managerial discipline, and the Spanish payout ratios are above the ones of the most developed countries.

The external mechanisms of control, basically the market for corporate control, are less important than in the Anglo-Saxon environment. The low number of listed companies, along with the relative illiquidity of the market reduce the informativeness of the stock prices and decreases significantly the possibility of success of takeovers. Another factor that reduces the functioning of the market for corporate control is the usually concentrated ownership structure and the implementation of some control-enhancing mechanism as means to increase the control power of the main shareholder among Spanish firms.

In the very moment, when this book is in print there are some shifts in the Spanish corporate governance that deserves at least a comment.

Despite considerable advances, we do not know yet what the best pattern of corporate governance both at a firm and a national level is. Furthermore, we do not have yet a clear view about how these two levels of corporate governance interact. In general, the attention of regulators, shareholders, and directors has shifted in the past 10 years. Although in the first years of this century the focus was on accounting, the financial crisis which begun in 2007 has led to a rising importance of the risk management. Thus, a highly controversial and time pertinent question on corporate governance is whether companies have adequate risk controls and to what extent the executive compensation can encourage wrong corporate risk taking.

The Spanish Government has recently appointed a special committee for the reform of the corporate governance in the country. The conclusions and suggestions of this committee are likely to translate into forthcoming laws or even a new Code of Good Governance. In January 2014, the Government announced the project of a new Company's Act Law, which will broaden the function of the Shareholders' General Meeting, deliver to directors more control over the corporate risk taking, and will tie the directors' compensation to the long-term performance and sustainability.

This view is in line with a rethink of the executive compensation principles, which emphasize a focus on *pay for performance* and the integration of risk management functions into the executive compensation structure. It is also consistent with the implementation of shareholders say-on-pay votes. The principle underlying say-on-pay is that shareholders must have the opportunity to express their views on the compensation decisions and on the policies of the companies. The say-on-pay is an important part of an ongoing, integrated engagement process between shareholders and boards, and can be the primary communication tool for shareholders expressing dissatisfaction with compensation practices.

As we can see, the Spanish corporate governance is moving forward as it does in most of the countries. Most of the stakeholders agree that a good corporate governance system is the cornerstone of an economic system oriented toward growth, employment, value creation, and sustainability. There is a number of challenges that should be addressed in the coming years, and new efforts to design well-functioning mechanism that avoids the repetition of new crisis episodes partially due to the failure of the corporate governance are vital.

References

Allen, F., and D. Gale. 2001. *Comparing Financial Systems.* Cambridge, MA: MIT Press.

Andrés, P., V. Azofra, and F. Tejerina. 2010. "The Bank: Controller or Predator in the Governance of Nonfinancial Firms?" *Investment Management and Financial Innovations* 7, no. 1, pp. 24–36.

Azofra, V. 2004. "El Gobierno De La Empresa En Perspectiva Internacional." In *El Gobierno De La Empresa. En Busca De La Transparencia Y La Confianza,* ed. E.B. Campos, 95–113. Madrid: Pirámide.

Bank of Spain. 2013. *www.bde.es*

Beck, T., A. Demirgüc-Kunt, and R. Levine. 2001. "The Financial Structure Database." In *Financial Structure & Economic Growth: A Cross-Country Comparison of Banks, Markets, & Development,* eds. A. Demirgüc-Kunt, and R. Levine, 17–80. Cambridge, MA: MIT Press.

Bergés, Á., and E. Sánchez del Villar. 1991. "Las Participaciones Bursátiles De La Banca En España." *Papeles de Economía Española* 34, pp. 72–86.

Blanch, J.A., A. Garrido Torres, and E. Sanromá. 1990. "Las Relaciones Banca-Industria Y Su Incidencia Sobre La Eficiencia Bancaria." *Economía Industrial* 272, pp. 85–94.

Blom, J., and M.B.J. Schauten. 2008. "Corporate Governance and the Cost of Debt." In *New Developments in Financial Modeling,* eds. J. Soares, J. Pina, and M. Calalao-Lopes. Cambridge Scholars Publishing, pp. 116–145.

Bloomfield, S., 2013. *Theory and Practice of Corporate Governance. An Integrated Approach.* New York, NY: Cambridge University Press.

Bolsas y Mercados Españoles. 2013. *Market Report 2012.* Madrid: Bolsas y Mercados Españoles.

Bolsas y Mercados Españoles, 2014. *Market Report 2013.* Madrid: Bolsas y Mercados Españoles.

Burkhart, M., F. Panunzi, and A. Shleifer. 2003. "Family Firms." *Journal of Finance* 58, pp. 2167–2201.

Cadbury Report. 1992. *Report of the Committee on the Financial Aspects of Corporate Governance.* European Corporate Governance Institute.

Cajigas García-Inés, J.M., and P. López Muñoz. 2013. "Spain Chapter—Corporate Governance 2013." In *Corporate Governance 2013,* eds. B. Hanton, and V. Marrison. London: International Comparative Legal Guides.

Casasola, M.J., M. Sanmartín, and J.A. Tribó. 2001. "La Participación Bancaria En Estructuras Con Varios Grandes Accionistas." *Economía Industrial* 341, pp. 43–53.

Chuliá, C. 1990. "Las Participaciones Del Sistema Bancario En Las Empresas No Financieras." *Papeles de Economía Española* 44, pp. 73–86.

Claessens, S., S. Djankov, J.P.H. Fan, and L.H.P. Lang. 2002. "Disentangling the Incentive and Entrenchment Effects of Large Shareholdings." *Journal of Finance* 57, pp. 2741–2771.

CNMV. 2011. *Corporate Report.* Madrid: Comisión Nacional del Mercado de Valores.

Conde, V. 2013. "Spain Chapter—Mergers and Acquisitions 2013." In *Mergers and Acquisitions 2013,* ed. M. Hatchard. London: International Comparative Legal Guides.

Cremers, K.J.M., V.B. Nair, and C. Wei. 2007. "Governance Mechanism and Bond Prices." *Review of Financial Studies* 20, pp. 1359–88.

Crespí, R., and M.A. García Cestona. 2002. "Ownership and Control of Spanish Listed Firms." In *The Control of Corporate Europe*, eds. F. Barca, and M. Becht. 207–227. Oxford: Oxford University Press.

Crespo, C. 2012. *Estudio De La Concentración Del Mercado De La Auditoría En España Y Su Evolución.* Valencia: Universidad Politécnica de Valencia.

Cronqvist, H., and M. Nilsson. 2003. "Agency Costs of Controlling Minority Shareholders." *Journal of Financial and Quantitative Analysis* 38, pp. 695–719.

Cuervo García, A. 2002. "Corporate Governance Mechanisms: A Plea for Less Code of Good Governance and More Market Control." *Corporate Governance: An International Review* 10, pp. 84–93.

Demirgüc-Kunt, A., and R. Levine. 2001. "Bank-Based & Market-Based Financial Systems: Cross-Country Comparisons." In *Financial Structure & Economic Growth: A Cross-Country Comparison of Banks, Markets, & Development*, eds. A. Demirgüc-Kunt, and R. Levine, 81–140. Cambridge, MA: MIT Press.

Demsetz, H., and K. Lehn. 1985. "The Structure of Corporate Ownership: Causes and Consequences." *Journal of Political Economy* 93, pp. 1155–1177.

Denis, D.K., and J.J. McConnell. 2003. "International Corporate Governance." *Journal of Financial and Quantitative Analysis* 38, pp. 1–36.

Dittmann, I., E. Maug, and C. Schneider. 2010. "Bankers on the Boards of German Firms: What They Do, What They are Worth, and Why They are (Still) There." *Review of Finance* 14, pp. 35–71.

Djankov, S., R. La Porta, F. Lopez-de-Silanes, and A. Shleifer. 2008. "The Law and Economics of Self-Dealing." *Journal of Financial Economics* 88, pp. 430–465.

Economist Intelligence Unit. 2010. *Industry Report: Spain Financial Services Report.* London: The Economis.

Enriques, L., and P. Volpin. 2007. "Corporate Governance Reforms in Continental Europe." *Journal of Economic Perspectives* 21, pp. 117–140.

Faccio, M., and L.H.P. Lang. 2002. "The Ultimate Ownership of Western European Corporations." *Journal of Financial Economics* 65, pp. 365–395.

Fernández, A.I., S. Gómez Ansón, and C. Fernández-Méndez. 1998. "The Effect of the Board Size and Composititon on Corporate Governance." In *Corporate Governance, Financial Markets and Global Convergence*, M. Balling, E. Hennessy, and R. O'Brien. Dordrecht: Kluwer Academic Publishers.

Fundación de Estudios Financieros. 2011. "Observatorio de Gobierno Corporativo 2010." In *Papeles de la Fundación n. 40. Madrid.*

García Blandón, J., and J.M. Argilés Bosch. 2013. Audit Firm Tenure and Qualified Opinions: New Evidence From Spain. Revista de Contabilidad—Spanish Accounting Review Forthcoming.

García-Castro, R., and R. Aguilera. 2012. "A Decade of Corporate Governance Reforms in Spain (2000–2010)." In *The Convergence of Corporate Governance: Promise and Prospects*, ed. H. Basingstoke. Palgrave Macmillan.

García Cestona, M.Á., J. Surroca, and J.A. Tribó Giné. 2005. "Evolución de la Relación Banca-Industria en España." In *Documentos de Trabajo. Serie Economía de la Empresa.* Universidad Carlos III.

García Meca, E., and J.P. Sánchez Ballesta. 2009. "Corporate Governance and Earnings Management: A Meta-Analysis." *Corporate Governance: An International Review* 17, pp. 594–610.

Gispert, C. 1998. "Board Turnover and Firm Performance in Spanish Companies." *Investigaciones Económicas* 22, pp. 517–536.

Gómez Ansón, S., and L. Cabeza García. 2009. "Spanish Codes of Good Governance: Lessons Learned, Present Situation and Future Expectations." In *Codes of Good Governance Around the World*, ed. F.J. López Iturriaga, 367–382. New York, NY: Nova Publishers.

Gonzalo Angulo, J.A. 2004. "Influencias Recíprocas Entre Información Financiera y Gobernanza Empresarial." In *El Gobierno de la Empresa. En Busca de la Transparencia y la Confianza*, ed. E. Bueno Campos, 277–311. Madrid: Pirámide.

Institutional Shareholder Services (ISS). 2007. Report on the *Proportionality Principle in the European Union.* External Study Commissioned by the European Commission.

Jensen, M.C. 1993. "The Modern Industrial Revolution, Exit, and the Failure of Internal Control Systems." *Journal of Finance* 48, pp. 831–880.

Krishnaswami, S., P.A. Spindt, and V. Subramaniam. 1999. "Information Asymmetry, Monitoring and the Placement Structure of Corporate Debt." *Journal of Financial Economics* 51, pp. 407–434.

La Porta, R., F. López de Silanes, and A. Shleifer. 2006. "What Works in Securities Laws?" *Journal of Finance* 61, pp. 1–31.

La Porta, R., F. López de Silanes, A. Shleifer, and R. Vishny. 1998. "Law and Finance." *Journal of Political Economy* 106, pp. 1113–55.

La Porta, R., F. López de Silanes, A. Shleifer, and R. Vishny. 2000a. "Agency Problems and Dividend Policies Around the World." *Journal of Finance* 55, pp. 1–33.

La Porta, R., F. López de Silanes, A. Shleifer, and R. Vishny. 2000b. "Investor Protection and Corporate Governance." *Journal of Financial Economics* 58, pp. 3–27.

Le Vourc'h, J., and P. Morand. 2011. *Study on the Effects of the Implementation of the Acquis on Statutory Audits of Annual and Consolidated Accountis Incluidng the Consequence of the Audit Market.* Paris: ESCP.

Leech, D., and M. Manjón. March 2002. "Corporate Governance in Spain (with an application of the Power Indices Approach)." *European Journal of Law and Economics* 13, no. 2, pp. 157–73.

Lehn, K.M., S. Patro, and M. Zhao. 2009. "Determinants of the Size and Composition of U.S. Corporate Boards: 1935–2000." *Financial Management* 48, pp. 747–80.

Levine, R. 2002. "Bank-Based or Market-Based Financial Systems: Which Is Better?" *Journal of Financial Intermediation* 11, pp. 398–428.

Li, J., and J.R. Harrison. 2008. "National Culture and the Composition and Leadership Structure of Boards of Directors." *Corporate Governance: An International Review* 16, pp. 375–85.

López Iturriaga, F.J. 2005. "Debt Ownership Structure and Legal System: An International Analysis." *Applied Economics* 37, pp. 355–65.

Manghetti, G. 2011. "Do Savings Banks Differ From Traditional Commercial Banks?" In *200 Years of Savings Banks: A Strong and Lasting Business Model for Responsible, Regional Retail Banking*, eds. Group WSBIESB, 141–56.

Miguel, A., and J. Pindado. 2001. "Determinants of Capital Structure: New Evidence From Spanish Panel Data." *Journal of Corporate Finance* 7.

Miller, M.H., and F. Modigliani. 1961. "Dividend Policy, Growth, and the Valuation of Shares." *Journal of Business* 34, pp. 411–33.

Mínguez, A., and J.F. Martín Ugedo. 2005. "Afectan las características del consejo de administración a su labor supervisora? Nueva evidencia para el mercado español." *Revista Europea de Dirección y Economía de la Empresa* 14, pp. 55–74.

Monterrey, J., and A. Sánchez. 2008. "Gobierno Corporativo, Conflictos de Agencia y Elección de Auditor." *Revista Española de Financiación y Contabilidad* 37, pp. 113–56.

Morgan Stanley Capital Investment. 2013. *MSCI High Dividend Yield Indices.* Morgan Stanley.

Nieto Sánchez, M.J., and J.A. Tribó Giné. 2000. "Determinantes de la Emisión de Deuda Negociable en las Empresas Españolas." *Revista Europea de Dirección y Economía de la Empresa* 9, pp. 61–80.

Pes, Á. 1990. "Banca Privada y Empresas no Financieras Durante Los Años 80." *Economía Industrial* 272, pp. 75–84.

PricewaterhouseCoopers. 2013. *Consejos de Administración de empresas cotizadas.* Madrid: PwC.

Rajan, R., and L. Zingales. 1995. "What Do We Know About Capital Structure? Some Evidence From International Data." *Journal of Finance* 50, pp. 1421–60.

Ruiz Barbadillo, E., N. Gómez Aguilar, and N. Carrera Pena. 2009. "Derogación de la Rotación Obligatoria de Auditores y Calidad de la Auditoría." *Revista de Economía Aplicada* 49, pp. 105–34.

Ruiz Mallorquí, M.V., and D.J. Santana Martín. 2009. "Ultimate Institutional Owner and Takeover Defenses in the Controlling Versus Minority Shareholders Context." *Corporate Governance: An International Review* 17, pp. 238–54.

Sáez, F.J., and M. Martín. 2000. "Las Participaciones Empresariales de la Banca y las Cajas de Ahorro Españolas, 1992–1998." *Papeles de Economía Española* 84–85, pp. 222–36.

Santana, D.J., and I. Aguiar. 2006. "El Último Propietario de las Empresas Cotizadas Españolas (1996–2002)." *Cuadernos de Economía y Dirección de la Empresa* 26, pp. 47–72.

Santana Martín, D.J. 2010. "Shareholders Coalitions in Spain." *Universia Business Review* 28, pp. 46–61.

Santana Martín, D.J., and I. Aguiar Díaz. 2007. *Una Década de Blindaje en España. 1996–2005.* Madrid: Comisión Nacional del Mercado de Valores.

Schauten, M., and D.J.C. van Dijk. 2011. "Corporate Governance and the Cost of Debt of Large European Firms." In *Report Series ERIM* (Ed.).

Schneider-Lenné, E.R. 1992. "Corporate Control in Germany." *Oxford Review of Economic Policy* 8, pp. 11–23.

Shleifer, A., and R. Vishny. 1997. "A Survey of Corporate Governance." *Journal of Finance* 52, pp. 737–82.

Shleifer, A., and R.W. Vishny. 1986. "Large Shareholders and Corporate Control." *Journal of Political Economy* 94, pp. 461–88.

Spencer Stuart. 2002. *Indice Spencer Stuart de Consejos de Administración. España.* Madrid: Spencer Stuart.

Tejerina, F., 2006. *The Influence of Banks on the Corporate Governance of Non-Financial Firms.* In Unpublished PhD dissertation. University of Valladolid.

Torrero, A. 1991. *Relaciones Banca-Industria. La Experiencia Española.* Madrid: Espasa Calpe.

World Economic Forum. 2014. Global Competitiveness Report 2013–2014. World Economic Forum.

Index

OTHER TITLES IN CORPORATE GOVERNANCE COLLECTION

William Q. Judge, Old Dominion University and Kenneth A. Merchant, University of Southern California, Collection Editors

- *A Director's Guide to Corporate Financial Reporting* by Kristen Fiolleau, Kris Hoang, and Karim Jamal
- *Blind Spots, Biases, and Other Pathologies in the Boardroom* by Kenneth A. Merchant and Katharina Pick
- *A Primer on Corporate Governance, Second Edition* by Cornelis A. de Kluyver

Business Expert Press has over 30 collection in business subjects such as finance, marketing strategy, sustainability, public relations, economics, accounting, corporate communications, and many others. For more information about all our collections, please visit www.businessexpertpress.com/collections.

Announcing the Business Expert Press Digital Library

Concise E-books Business Students Need for Classroom and Research

This book can also be purchased in an e-book collection by your library as

- a one-time purchase,
- that is owned forever,
- allows for simultaneous readers,
- has no restrictions on printing, and
- can be downloaded as PDFs from within the library community.

Our digital library collections are a great solution to beat the rising cost of textbooks. E-books can be loaded into their course management systems or onto students' e-book readers.

The **Business Expert Press** digital libraries are very affordable, with no obligation to buy in future years. For more information, please visit **www.businessexpertpress.com/librarians**. To set up a trial in the United States, please email **sales@businessexpertpress.com.**

www.ingramcontent.com/pod-product-compliance
Lightning Source LLC
Chambersburg PA
CBHW071909200326
41519CB00016B/4544

9781606497609